Learning HTTP/2
A Practical Guide for Beginners

D0879105

Stephen Ludin and Javier Garza

Beijing · Boston · Farnham · Sebastopol · Tokyo

Learning HTTP/2

by Stephen Ludin and Javier Garza

Copyright © 2017 Stephen Ludin, Javier Garza. All rights reserved.

Printed in the United States of America.

Published by O'Reilly Media, Inc., 1005 Gravenstein Highway North, Sebastopol, CA 95472.

O'Reilly books may be purchased for educational, business, or sales promotional use. Online editions are also available for most titles (*http://oreilly.com/safari*). For more information, contact our corporate/institutional sales department: 800-998-9938 or *corporate@oreilly.com*.

Acquisitions Editor: Brian Anderson	**Indexer:** Wendy Catalano
Editors: Virginia Wilson and Dawn Schanafelt	**Interior Designer:** David Futato
Production Editor: Shiny Kalapurakkel	**Cover Designer:** Karen Montgomery
Copyeditor: Kim Cofer	**Illustrator:** Rebecca Demarest
Proofreader: Sonia Saruba	

June 2017:   First Edition

Revision History for the First Edition

2017-05-14:   First Release

See *http://oreilly.com/catalog/errata.csp?isbn=9781491962442* for release details.

978-1-491-96244-2

[LSI]

Table of Contents

Preface

HTTP/2, also called h2 for simplicity, is a major revision of the HTTP network protocol used by the World Wide Web, meant to improve the perceived performance of loading web content.

Since HTTP/1.1 (h1) was approved in 1999, the web has changed significantly from mostly text-based web pages that weighed a few kilobytes and included less than 10 objects, to today's media-rich websites that weigh on average over 2 megabytes,[1] and include an average of 140 objects. However, the HTTP protocol used to deliver the web content did not change in the intervening years, making room for a new industry of Web Performance experts who specialize in coming up with workarounds to help the aging protocol load web pages faster. People's expectations for performance have changed too—while in the late '90s people were willing to wait up to seven seconds for a page to load, a 2009 study by Forrester Research found that online shoppers expected pages to load under two seconds, with a large share of users abandoning sites where pages take over three seconds to load. A recent study by Google showed that a even a delay of 400 milliseconds (the blink of an eye) will cause people to search less.

That's why h2 was created—a protocol that can better handle today's complex pages without sacrificing speed. HTTP/2's adoption has been increasing[2] as more website administrators realize they can improve the perceived performance of their websites with little effort.

We all use h2 every day—it powers some of the most popular sites like Facebook, Twitter, Google, and Wikipedia—but many people don't know about it. Our goal is to educate you on h2 and its performance benefits, so you can get the most out of it.

---

1 *http://bit.ly/2oEc8sA*

2 *http://bit.ly/2pNKiL4*

Who Should Read This Book

Regardless of your role, if you find yourself responsible for any part of the life cycle of a website, this book will be useful for you. It is intended for people building or running websites, and in general anybody considering implementing h2, or looking to understand how it works.

We expect you to be familiar with web browsers, web servers, websites, and the basics of the HTTP protocol.

What This Book Isn't

The goal of this book is to teach you h2 and help you make the most out of the new version of the HTTP protocol. It is not a comprehensive guide for all h2 clients, servers, debug tools, performance benchmarking, etc. This book is intended for people not familiar with HTTP/2, but even experts may still find it to be a convenient resource.

Recommended Resources

h2book.com (*https://h2book.com*) is the companion website of this book, where you will find some of the examples referenced in later chapters. In addition, we recommend the following books:

- *High Performance Websites*, by Steve Souders (O'Reilly): Essential knowledge for frontend engineers
- *Even Faster Websites*, by Steve Souders (O'Reilly): Performance best practices for web developers
- *High Performance Browser Networking*, by Ilya Grigorik (O'Reilly): Hands-on overview about the various types of networks, transport protocols, application protocols, and APIs available in the browser
- *Using WebPageTest*, by Rick Viscomi, Andy Davies, and Marcel Duran (O'Reilly): Learn basic and advanced uses of WebPagetest, a free performance measurement tool for optimizing websites
- *High Performance Mobile Web*, by Maximiliano Firtman (O'Reilly): Optimize the performance of your mobile websites and webapps
- *http2 explained* (*https://daniel.haxx.se/http2/*), by Daniel Stenberg

Conventions Used in This Book

The following typographical conventions are used in this book:

Italic

> Indicates new terms, URLs, email addresses, filenames, and file extensions.

`Constant width`

> Used for program listings, as well as within paragraphs to refer to program elements such as variable or function names, databases, data types, environment variables, statements, and keywords.

`Constant width bold`

> Shows commands or other text that should be typed literally by the user.

`Constant width italic`

> Shows text that should be replaced with user-supplied values or by values determined by context.

 This icon signifies a tip, suggestion, or general note.

 This icon indicates a warning or caution.

Using Code Examples

Supplemental material (code examples, exercises, etc.) is available for download at *https://github.com/oreillymedia/learning-http2*.

This book is here to help you get your job done. In general, if example code is offered with this book, you may use it in your programs and documentation. You do not need to contact us for permission unless you're reproducing a significant portion of the code. For example, writing a program that uses several chunks of code from this book does not require permission. Selling or distributing a CD-ROM of examples from O'Reilly books does require permission. Answering a question by citing this book and quoting example code does not require permission. Incorporating a significant amount of example code from this book into your product's documentation does require permission.

We appreciate, but do not require, attribution. An attribution usually includes the title, author, publisher, and ISBN. For example: "*Learning HTTP/2* by Stephen Ludin and Javier Garza (O'Reilly). Copyright 2017 Stephen Ludin and Javier Garza, 978-1-491-96244-2."

If you feel your use of code examples falls outside fair use or the permission given above, feel free to contact us at *permissions@oreilly.com*.

O'Reilly Safari

 *Safari* (formerly Safari Books Online) is a membership-based training and reference platform for enterprise, government, educators, and individuals.

Members have access to thousands of books, training videos, Learning Paths, interactive tutorials, and curated playlists from over 250 publishers, including O'Reilly Media, Harvard Business Review, Prentice Hall Professional, Addison-Wesley Professional, Microsoft Press, Sams, Que, Peachpit Press, Adobe, Focal Press, Cisco Press, John Wiley & Sons, Syngress, Morgan Kaufmann, IBM Redbooks, Packt, Adobe Press, FT Press, Apress, Manning, New Riders, McGraw-Hill, Jones & Bartlett, and Course Technology, among others.

For more information, please visit *http://oreilly.com/safari*.

How to Contact Us

Please address comments and questions concerning this book to the publisher:

> O'Reilly Media, Inc.
> 1005 Gravenstein Highway North
> Sebastopol, CA 95472
> 800-998-9938 (in the United States or Canada)
> 707-829-0515 (international or local)
> 707-829-0104 (fax)

We have a web page for this book, where we list errata, examples, and any additional information. You can access this page at *http://oreil.ly/2q2TrBm*.

To comment or ask technical questions about this book, send email to *bookquestions@oreilly.com*.

For more information about our books, courses, conferences, and news, see our website at *http://www.oreilly.com*.

Find us on Facebook: *http://facebook.com/oreilly*

Follow us on Twitter: *http://twitter.com/oreillymedia*

Watch us on YouTube: *http://www.youtube.com/oreillymedia*

Acknowledgments

We would like to thank Akamai's h2 core team and Moritz Steiner, one of Akamai's researchers on the Foundry team who coauthored several h2 papers with Stephen; Pierre Lermant (for his good sense of humor, attention to detail, and his contribution for reviewing and contributing content for this book); Martin Flack (for his often illuminating Lisp implementation and also a member of Akamai's Foundry team); Jeff Zitomer (for his support, encouragement, and contagious smile); Mark Nottingham (for his contributions to the h2 protocol); Pat Meenan (for all the countless contributions to Webpagetest.org, probably the best free tool for Measuring Web Performance); and Andy Davies (who created the "WebPagetest Bulk Tester," which we used extensively across this book).

Thanks to our editors Brian Anderson, Virginia Wilson, and Dawn Schanafelt for making everything so easy, and all the h2 experts who provided feedback and ideas for this book: Ilya Grigorik, Patrick McManus, Daniel Stenberg, Ragnar Lonn, Colin Bendell, Mark Nottingham, Hooman Beheshti, Rob Trace, Tim Kadlec, and Pat Meenan.

Javier Garza

Above all, I would like to thank my wife Tina for her support, encouragement, and understanding. Thanks to my dear kids (Keona, Diego, and Lani) for still showing me their love every day even after spending countless nights, weekends, and a big chunk of our summer vacation writing this book. Thank you also to my managers Aditi and Austin for their encouragment to write this book on top of a very demanding job.

Stephen Ludin

Patience. I want to acknowledge patience. The patience of my family: Sarah, Tomas, and Liam for putting up with me and this crazy process of publishing. Their support was invaluable throughout my writing. The patience of my employer, Akamai, allowing me to make time in an always busy schedule to work on this book. The patience of O'Reilly for the practiced understanding that for their team of authors, writing a book is inevitably a third job. Lastly, the patience of my parents who gave me a leg up that I can never pay back, but can only pay forward—when my dad brought home an Atari 800 when I was nine, did he know it would propel me on a course whose destination (I like to think) still lies before me?

Foreword

In 2009, HTTP/1.1 was well over a decade old, and arguably still the most popular application protocol on the internet. Not only was it used for browsing the web, it was the go-to protocol for a multitude of other things. Its ease of use, broad implementation, and widely shared understanding by developers and operation engineers gave it huge advantages, and made it hard to replace. Some people were even starting to say that it formed a "second waist" for the classic hourglass model of the internet's architecture.

However, HTTP was showing its age. The web had changed tremendously in its lifetime, and its demands strained the venerable protocol. Now loading a single web page often involved making hundreds of requests, and their collective overhead was slowing down the web. As a result, a whole cottage industry of Web Performance Optimization started forming to create workarounds.

These problems were seen clearly in the HTTP community, but we didn't have the mandate to fix them; previous efforts like HTTP-NG had failed, and without strong support for a proposal from both web browsers and servers, it felt foolish to start a speculative effort. This was reflected in the HTTP working group's charter at the time, which said:

> The Working Group must not introduce a new version of HTTP and should not add new functionality to HTTP.

Instead, our mission was to clarify HTTP's specification, and (at least for me) to rebuild a strong community of HTTP implementers.

That said, there was still interest in more efficient expressions of HTTP's semantics, such as Roy Fielding's WAKA proposal[1] (which unfortunately has never been completed) and work on HTTP over SCTP[2] (primarily at the University of Delaware).

Sometime after giving a talk at Google that touched on some of these topics, I got a note from Mike Belshe, asking if we could meet. Over dinner on Castro Street in Mountain View, he sketched out that Google was about to announce an HTTP replacement protocol called SPDY.

SPDY was different because Mike worked on the Chrome browser, and he was paired with Roberto Peon, who worked on GFE, Google's frontend web server. Controlling both ends of the connection allowed them to iterate quickly, and testing the protocol on Google's massive traffic allowed them to verify the design at scale.

I spent a lot of that dinner with a broad smile on my face. They were solving real problems, had running code and data from it. These are all things that the Internet Engineering Task Force (IETF) loves.

However, it wasn't until 2012 that things really began to take off for SPDY; Firefox implemented the new protocol, followed by the Nginx server, followed by Akamai. Netcraft reported a surge in the number of sites supporting SPDY.

It was becoming obvious that there was broad interest in a new version of HTTP.

In October 2012, the HTTP working group was re-chartered to publish HTTP/2, using SPDY as a starting point. Over the next two years, representatives of various companies and open source projects met all over the world to talk about this new protocol, resolve issues, and assure that their implementations interoperated.

In that process, we had several disagreements and even controversies. However, I remain impressed by the professionalism, willingness to engage, and good faith demonstrated by everyone in the process; it was a remarkable group to work with.

For example, in a few cases it was agreed that moving forward was more important than one person's argument carrying the day, so we made decisions by flipping a coin. While this might seem like madness to some, to me it demonstrates maturity and perspective that's rare.

In December 2014, just 16 days over our chartered deadline (which is early, at least in standards work), we submitted HTTP/2 to the Internet Engineering Steering Group for approval.

---

1 *https://tools.ietf.org/agenda/83/slides/slides-83-httpbis-5.pdf*

2 *https://tools.ietf.org/html/draft-natarajan-http-over-sctp-00*

The proof, as they say, is in the pudding; in the IETF's case, "running code." We quickly had that, with support in all of the major browsers, and multiple web servers, CDNs, and tools.

HTTP/2 is by no means perfect, but that was never our intent. While the immediate goal was to clear the cobwebs and improve web performance incrementally, the bigger goal was to "prime the pump" and assure that we *could* successfully introduce a new version of HTTP, so that the web doesn't get stuck on an obsolete protocol.

By that measure, it's easy to see that we succeeded. And, of course, we're not done yet.

— *Mark Nottingham*

Mark Nottingham has been involved with the HTTP Working Group for over 10 years. Significantly for this book, he was the Working Group chair while HTTP/2 was developed. He currently serves as the Working Group chair for QUIC and is a former member of Akamai's Foundry team.

CHAPTER 1

The Evolution of HTTP

In the 1930s, Vannevar Bush, an electrical engineer from the United States then at MIT's School of Engineering, had a concern with the volume of information people were producing relative to society's ability to consume that information. In his essay published in the *Atlantic Monthly* in 1945 entitled, "As We May Think," he said:

> Professionally our methods of transmitting and reviewing the results of research are generations old and by now are totally inadequate for their purpose. If the aggregate time spent in writing scholarly works and in reading them could be evaluated, the ratio between these amounts of time might well be startling.

He envisioned a system where our aggregate knowledge was stored on microfilm and could be "consulted with exceeding speed and flexibility." He further stated that this information should have contextual associations with related topics, much in the way the human mind links data together. His *memex* system was never built, but the ideas influenced those that followed.

The term *Hypertext* that we take for granted today was coined around 1963 and first published in 1965 by Ted Nelson, a software designer and visionary. He proposed the concept of hypertext to mean:

> ...a body of written or pictorial material interconnected in such a complex way that it could not conveniently be presented or represented on paper. It may contain summaries, or maps of its contents and their interrelations; it may contain annotations, additions and footnotes from scholars who have examined it. [1]

Nelson wanted to create a "docuverse" where information was interlinked and never deleted and easily available to all. He built on Bush's ideas and in the 1970s created a

---

1 T. H. Nelson. "Complex information processing: a file structure for the complex, the changing and the indeterminate." ACM '65 Proceedings of the 1965 20th national conference.

prototype implementation of a hypertext system with his project Xanadu. It was unfortunately never completed, but provided the shoulders to stand on for those to come.

HTTP enters the picture in 1989. While at CERN, Tim Berners-Lee proposed[2] a new system for helping keep track of the information created by "the accelerators" (referencing the yet-to-be-built Large Hadron Collider) and experiments at the institution. He embraces two concepts from Nelson: Hypertext, or "Human-readable information linked together in an unconstrained way," and Hypermedia, a term to "indicate that one is not bound to text." In the proposal he discussed the creation of a server and browsers on many machines that could provide a "universal system."

HTTP/0.9 and 1.0

HTTP/0.9 was a wonderfully simple, if limited, protocol. It had a single method (GET), there were no headers, and it was designed to only fetch HTML (meaning no images—just text).

Over the next few years, use of HTTP grew. By 1995 there were over 18,000 servers handling HTTP traffic on port 80 across the world. The protocol had evolved well past its 0.9 roots, and in 1996 RFC 1945[3] codified HTTP/1.0.

Version 1.0 brought a massive amount of change to the little protocol that started it all. Whereas the 0.9 *spec* was about a page long, the 1.0 RFC came in at 60 pages. You could say it had grown from a toy into a tool. It brought in ideas that are very familiar to us today:

- Headers
- Response codes
- Redirects
- Errors
- Conditional requests
- Content encoding (compression)
- More request methods

and more. HTTP/1.0, though a large leap from 0.9, still had a number of known flaws that had to be addressed—most notably, the inability to keep a connection open between requests, the lack of a mandatory Host header, and bare bones options for

---

2 *https://www.w3.org/History/1989/proposal.html*

3 *https://tools.ietf.org/html/rfc1945*

caching. These three items had consequences on how the web could scale and needed to be addressed.

HTTP/1.1

Right on the heels of 1.0 came 1.1, the protocol that has lived on for over 20 years. It fixed a number of the aforementioned 1.0 problems. By making the Host header mandatory, it was now possible to perform *virtual hosting*, or serving multiple web properties on a singe IP address. When the new connection directives are used, a web server is not required to close a connection after a response. This was a boon for performance and efficiency since the browser no longer needed to reestablish the TCP connection on every request.

Additional changes included:

- An extension of cacheability headers
- An OPTIONS method
- The Upgrade header
- Range requests
- Compression with transfer-encoding
- Pipelining

 Pipelining is a feature that allows a client to send all of its requests at once. There were a couple of problems with pipelining that prevented its popularity. Servers still had to respond to the requests in order. This meant if one request takes a long time, this *head of line blocking* will get in the way of the other requests. Additionally, pipelining implementations in servers and proxies on the internet tended to range from nonexistent (bad) to broken (worse).

HTTP/1.1 was the result of HTTP/1.0's success and the experience gained running the older protocol for a few years.

RFCs for HTTP/1.1

The Internet Engineering Task Force (IETF) publishes protocol specifications in committee-created drafts called *Request for Comments* (RFC). These committees are open to anyone with the time and inclination to participate. HTTP/1.1 was first defined in RFC 2068, then later replaced by RFC 2616, and finally revised in RFCs 7230 through 7235.

Beyond 1.1

Since 1999, RFC 2616, which specified HTTP/1.1, has defined the standard that the modern web is built on. Written in stone, it did not evolve or change. The web, however, and the way we used it continued to change in ways likely unimagined by its originators. The interactivity and utility of your average commerce site go well beyond the vision of an interwoven docuverse and fundamentally change the way we participate in our world. That evolution came despite the limitation of the protocol that we see today.

The most tangible change we can point to is in the makeup of web pages. The HTTP Archives only goes back to 2010, but in even that relatively short time the change has been dramatic. Every added object adds complexity and strains a protocol designed to request one object at a time.

SPDY

In 2009, Mike Belshe and Roberto Peon of Google proposed an alternative to HTTP, which they called SPDY[4] (pronounced "speedy"). SPDY was not the first proposal to replace HTTP, but it was the most important as it moved the perceived performance mountain. Before SPDY, it was thought that there was not enough will in the industry to make breaking, or incompatible, changes to HTTP/1.1. The effort that would be required to coordinate the changes between browsers, servers, proxies, and various middle boxes was seen to be too great.

SPDY, however, changed everything. It quickly proved that there was a desire for something more efficient and a willingness to change. SPDY laid the groundwork for HTTP/2 and was responsible for proving out some of its key features such as multiplexing, framing, and header compression, among others. It was integrated quickly, even in internet time, into Chrome and Firefox, and eventually would be adopted by almost every major browser. Similarly, the necessary support in servers and proxies came along at about the same pace.

HTTP/2

In early 2012, the HTTP working group (the IETF group responsible for the HTTP specifications) was rechartered to work on the next version of HTTP. A key portion of its charter[5] laid out their expectations for this new protocol:

---

4 *http://bit.ly/2oi9ZS9*

5 *http://bit.ly/2oid6cP*

It is expected that HTTP/2.0 will:

- Substantially and measurably improve end-user perceived latency in most cases, over HTTP/1.1 using TCP.

- Address the "head of line blocking" problem in HTTP.

- Not require multiple connections to a server to enable parallelism, thus improving its use of TCP, especially regarding congestion control.

- Retain the semantics of HTTP/1.1, leveraging existing documentation (see above), including (but not limited to) HTTP methods, status codes, URIs, and header fields.

- Clearly define how HTTP/2.0 interacts with HTTP/1.x, especially in intermediaries (both 2->1 and 1->2).

- Clearly identify any new extensibility points and policy for their appropriate use.

A call for proposals was sent out and it was decided to use SDPY as a starting point for HTTP/2.0. Finally, on May 14, 2015, RFC 7540 was published and HTTP/2 was official.

The remainder of this book lays out the rest of the story.

CHAPTER 2

HTTP/2 Quick Start

When faced with something new and shiny, rarely do we want to spend the first hours meticulously going through the manual, reading the instructions, maintenance details, and safety advisories. We want to tear it out of the packaging, plug it in, turn it on, and start experiencing the wonders promised on the box. HTTP/2 (h2) should be no different.

So let's start tinkering.

Up and Running

Realistically, you have likely been experiencing HTTP/2 on a daily basis. Open a modern browser (e.g., Edge, Safari, Firefox, Chrome) and point it at a major website like Facebook, Instagram, or Twitter, and voila! you are using h2. Truth be told, this is likely anticlimactic and not the reason you are holding this book in your hands. Let's get things up and running so that *you* can be running the next major website over h2.

There are two major steps to getting an h2 server up and running:

- Get and install a web server that speaks h2
- Get and install a TLS certificate so the browser will speak h2 with the server

Neither of these are trivial, but we are going to try to make it as simple as possible. There is a more exhaustive treatment of the subject in "Servers, Proxies, and Caches" on page 94, but hopefully you will be running an h2 server by the end of this chapter.

Get a Certificate

Working with certificates is a subject that merits a book of its own. We are going to skip right through all of the theory and get a certificate in your hands for experimentation purposes as quickly as possible. We will explore three methods: using online resources, creating a cert on your own, and obtaining a cert from a Certificate Authority (CA)—we'll use Let's Encrypt in this case. It should be noted that the first two methods will create what is called a self-signed certificate, and are useful for testing purposes only. Since a self-signed cert is not signed by a CA, it will generate warnings in a web browser.

Use an Online Generator

There are a number of online resources for generating a self-signed certificate. Since you will not have generated the private key in your own secure environment, these certs should never be used for any purpose beyond experimentation like we are doing here. A web search will quickly get you to a couple of resources. One option is *https://www.sslchecker.com/csr/self_signed*.

Use the tool and save the generated certificate and key to two local files. Name the files *privkey.pem* and *cert.pem*, respectively, for now.

Self Signed

The openssl tool, available from *https://www.openssl.org*, is fairly universal and easily obtainable. There are ports for almost every major platform, and it is what we will use to show how to create a self-signed certificate and key. If you have a Unix/Linux or Mac OS flavor machine you very likely have this tool installed already. Fire up your terminal and repeat after me:

```
$ openssl genrsa -out key.pem 2048
$ openssl req -new -x509 -sha256 -key privkey.pem -out cert.pem -days 365 \
    -subj "/CN=fake.example.org"
```

With this you will have a new key called `privkey.pem` and a new cert called `cert.pem`.

Let's Encrypt

Let's Encrypt is a new player on the Certificate Authority scene, having gone live with its public beta in the fall of 2015. Its goal is to make TLS certificates available in an easy, automated, and inexpensive (free) manner to anyone and everyone. This is core to the *TLS Everywhere* movement, which can be summed up as the belief that all of our web communications should always be encrypted and authenticated. For our purposes here, the "easy" bit is what is attractive so we can get up and running as soon as possible.

Though there are now many clients and libraries to choose from[1] that integrate with Let's Encrypt, the Electronic Frontier Foundation (EFF) maintains the Let's Encrypt recommended client called certbot.[2] Certbot is intended to make certificate acquisition and maintenance a complete hands-off process by doing everything from obtaining the certificate and then installing the certificate on your web server for you.

 In order to obtain a certificate from Let's Encrypt, you will need to be able to validate your domain. This implies you have control of the domain and can prove it by modifying DNS or the web server. If you do not have a domain or do not want to be bothered, simply use the *self-signed* method shown previously.

Follow instructions for downloading certbot for your favorite operating system. For the purposes of this chapter you do not need to be concerned with the web server choice. For Linux flavors, the simplest method for most cases is to do the following on the machine running your web server:

```
$ wget https://dl.eff.org/certbot-auto
$ chmod a+x certbot-auto
```

Once downloaded, run `certbot-auto` like so:

```
$ ./certbot-auto certonly --webroot -w <your web root> -d <your domain>
```

substituting your web server filesystem root and your domain in the relevant places. This will automatically install any needed packages, prompt you with a number of questions, and finally, if all goes well, obtain the certificate from Let's Encrypt. Your newly minted cert and private keys will be placed in */etc/letsencrypt/live/<your domain>*:

File	Description
/etc/letsencrypt/live/<your domain>/privkey.pem	Your certificate's private key
/etc/letsencrypt/live/<your domain>/cert.pem	Your new certificate
/etc/letsencrypt/live/<your domain>/chain.pem	The Let's Encrypt CA chain
/etc/letsencrypt/live/<your domain>/fullchain.pem	Your new cert and the chain all in one

Get and Run Your First HTTP/2 Server

There are numerous choices for obtaining and running a web server that speaks HTTP/2. ("Servers, Proxies, and Caches" on page 94 describes several options.) Our

---

1 *https://community.letsencrypt.org/t/list-of-client-implementations/2103*

2 *https://certbot.eff.org/*

goal here is to be quick and simple, and for that we will look toward the nghttp2 package. nghttp2,[3] developed by Tatsuhiro Tsujikawa, provides a number of useful tools for working with and debugging h2. For now, we are interested in the `nghttpd` tool.

There is more information on nghttp2 in "nghttp2" on page 110, but we'll try to get you started here. Install nghttp2 via your favorite package manager or (for the brave) from the source. For example, on Ubuntu 16:

```
$ sudo apt-get install nghttp2
```

Once installed, with certificates in hand, run `nghttpd` as:

```
$ ./nghttpd -v -d <webroot> <port> <key> <cert>
```

where `<webroot>` is the path to your website, `<port>` is the port you want the server to listen to, and `<key>` and `<cert>` are paths to the key and certificate you generated. For example:

```
$ ./nghttpd -v -d /usr/local/www 8443 \
        /etc/letsencrypt/live/yoursite.com/privkey.pem \
        /etc/letsencrypt/live/yoursite.com/cert.pem
```

Pick a Browser

Finally, the reward for the hard work. Pick a modern browser and point it at your new server. See "Desktop Web Browsers" on page 91 for a very comprehensive list of browsers that support HTTP/2. If you created a self-signed certificate, you should see a security warning. Confirm that it is complaining about the cert you created, and accept the warnings. You should see your website now.

And it is being served over h2!

---

3 *https://nghttp2.org*

CHAPTER 3

How and Why We Hack the Web

Using a (relatively) ancient protocol to deliver fast modern web pages has become a virtual act of acrobatics. An entire specialty of web performance engineer has built up around it. One could argue that O'Reilly's Velocity conference series was born in part from people wanting to share their various tricks and hacks to get the most out of the venerable protocol. To understand where we are going (namely, toward HTTP/2), it is important to understand where we are, the challenges we face, and how we are dealing with them today.

Performance Challenges Today

Delivering a modern web page or web application is far from a trivial affair. With hundreds of objects per page, tens of domains, variability in the networks, and a wide range of device abilities, creating a consistent and fast web experience is a challenge. Understanding the steps involved in web page retrieval and rendering, as well as the challenges faced in those steps, is an important factor in creating something that does not get in the way of users interacting with your site. It also provides you with the insight needed to understand the motivations behind HTTP/2 and will allow you to evaluate the relative merits of its features.

The Anatomy of a Web Page Request

Before we dig in, it is important to have a baseline understanding of what we are trying to optimize; specifically, what goes on in the time between when users click a link in a web browser and the page being displayed on their screen. When a browser requests a web page, it goes through a repetitive process to get all of the information it needs to paint the page on the screen. It is easiest to think of this in two parts: the object fetching logic, and the page parsing/rendering logic. Let's start with fetching. Figure 3-1 shows the components of this process.

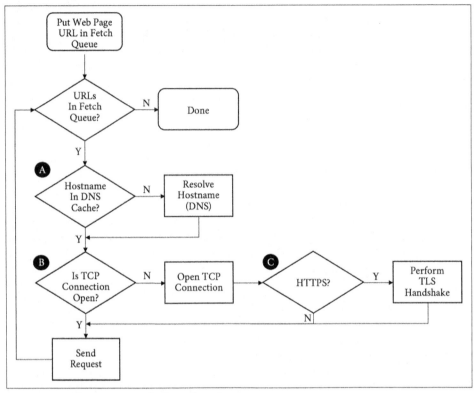

Figure 3-1. Object request/fetching flowchart

Walking through the flowchart, we:

1. Put the URL to fetch in the queue
2. Resolve the IP address of the hostname in the URL (A)
3. Open a TCP connection to the host (B)
4. If it is an HTTPS request, initiate and finish a TLS handshake (C)
5. Send the request for the base page URL

Figure 3-2 describes receiving the response and rendering the page.

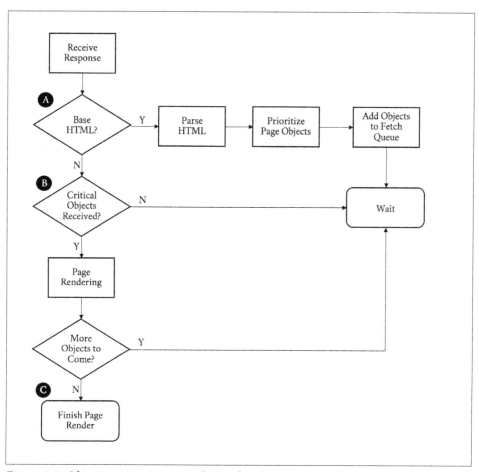

Figure 3-2. Object response/page rendering flowchart

Continuing on with our walk through the flowchart, we:

6. Receive the response
7. If this is the base HTML, parse it and trigger prioritized fetches for the objects on the page (A)
8. If the critical objects on a page have been received, start rendering (B)
9. As additional objects are received, continue to parse and render until done (C)

The preceding process needs to be repeated for every page click. It puts a strain on the network and device resources. Working to optimize or eliminate any of these steps is core to the art of web performance tuning.

Critical Performance

With the previous diagrams we can call out the areas that matter for web performance and where our challenges may start. Let's start with the network-level metrics that have an overall effect on the loading of a web page:

Latency

> The latency is how long it takes for an IP packet to get from one point to another. Related is the Round-Trip Time (RTT), which is twice the latency. Latency is a major bottleneck to performance, especially for protocols such as HTTP, which tend to make many round-trips to the server.

Bandwidth

> A connection between two points can only handle so much data at one time before it is saturated. Depending on the amount of data on a web page and the capacity of the connection, bandwidth may be a bottleneck to performance.

DNS lookup

> Before a client can fetch a web page, it needs to translate the hostname to an IP address using the Domain Name System (DNS), the internet's phone book (for the few of you readers who will understand the metaphor). This needs to happen for every unique hostname on the fetched HTML page as well, though luckily only once per hostname.

Connection time

> Establishing a connection requires a back and forth (round-trip) between the client and the server called the "three-way handshake." This handshake time is generally related to the latency between the client and the server. The handshake involves sending a synchronize (SYN) packet from the client to the server, followed by a acknowledgment (ACK) of that SYN from the server, a SYN packet from the server to the client, and an ACK of that SYN from the client to the server. See Figure 3-3.

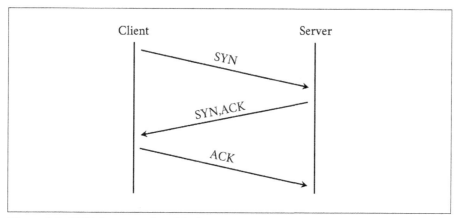

Figure 3-3. TCP three-way handshake

TLS negotiation time
> If the client is making an HTTPS connection, it needs to negotiate Transport Layer Security (TLS), the successor to Secure Socket Layer (SSL). This involves more round-trips on top of server and client processing time.

At this point the client has yet to even send the request and has already spent a DNS round-trip plus a few more for TCP and TLS. Next we have metrics that are more dependent on the content or the performance of the server itself as opposed to the network:

Time to First Byte
> TTFB is the measure of time from when the client starts the navigation to a web page until the first byte of the base page response is received. It is a sum of many of the preceding metrics as well as any server processing time. For objects on a page, TTFB measures the time from when the browser sends the request to the time the first byte comes back.

Content download time
> This is the Time to Last Byte (TTLB) for the requested object.

Start render time
> How quickly is the client able to start putting something on the screen for the user? This is the measurement of how long the user spends looking at a blank page.

Document complete (aka Page Load Time)
> This is the time that the page is considered *done* by the client.

When we look at web performance, especially if the goal is to create a new protocol that will make things faster, these are the metrics that must be kept in mind. We will reference these as we discuss the problems we face with HTTP/1.1 and why we might want something different.

With those metrics in mind you can see the internet's trend toward *more* of everything has led to performance bottlenecks. Here are some of the *mores* we need to keep in mind:

More bytes
> A truism is that every year pages are larger, images are larger, and JavaScript and CSS are larger. Larger means more bytes to download and longer *page load times*.

More objects
> Objects are not just larger, but there are many more of them. More objects can contribute to higher times overall as everything is fetched and processed.

More complexity
> Pages and their dependent objects are getting increasingly complex as we add more and richer functionality. With complexity, the time to calculate and render pages, especially on weaker mobile devices with less processing power, goes up.

More hostnames
> Pages are not fetched from individual hosts, and most pages have tens of referenced hosts. Each hostname means more *DNS lookups*, *connection times*, and *TLS negotiations*.

More TCP sockets
> In an effort to address some of these *mores*, clients open multiple sockets per hostname. This increases the per-host connection negotiation overhead, adds load to the device, and potentially overloads network connections, causing effective bandwidth to drop due to retransmits and bufferbloat.

The Problems with HTTP/1

HTTP/1 has gotten us to were we are today, but the demands of the modern web put focus on its design limitations. Following are some of the more significant issues the protocol faces, and consequently the core problems that HTTP/2 was designed to address.

 There is no such thing as HTTP/1. We are using that (and h1) as a shorthand for HTTP/1.0 (RFC 1945) and HTTP/1.1 (RFC 2616).

Head of line blocking

A browser rarely wants to get a single object from a particular host. More often it wants to get many objects at the same time. Think of a website that puts all of its images on a particular domain. HTTP/1 provides no mechanism to ask for those objects simultaneously. On a single connection it needs to send a request and then wait for a response before it can send another. h1 has a feature called pipelining that allows it to send a bunch of requests at once, but it will still receive the responses one after another in the order they were sent. Additionally, pipelining is plagued by various issues around interop and deployment that make its use impractical.

If any problems occur with any of those requests or responses, everything else gets blocked behind that request/response. This is referred to as *head of line blocking*. It can grind the transmission and rendering of a web page to a halt. To combat this, today's browser will open up to six connections to a particular host and send a request down each connection. This achieves a type of parallelism, but each connection can still suffer from head of line blocking. In addition, it is not a good use of limited device resources; the following section explains why.

Inefficient use of TCP

TCP (Transmission Control Protocol) was designed to be conservative in its assumptions and fair to the different traffic uses on a network. Its congestion avoidance mechanisms are built to work on the poorest of networks and be relatively fair in the presence of competing demand. That is one of the reasons it has been as successful as it has—not necessarily because it is the fastest way to transmit data, but because it is one of the most reliable. Central to this is a concept called the *congestion window*. The congestion window is the number of TCP packets that the sender can transmit out before being acknowledged by the receiver. For example, if the congestion window was set to one, the sender would transmit one packet, and only when it gets the receiver's acknowledgment of that packet would it send another.

What Is a Packet?

A packet, or more specifically an Internet Protocol (IP) packet, is a series of bytes (aka the payload) encapsulated in a structure (aka the frame) that defines how long the packet is, how it should be delivered (where it came from and where it is going), and other items needed to speak TCP. The most data we can effectively put in a packet's payload is 1460 bytes. Have an image that is (conveniently) 14,600 bytes in size? That will get split up into 10 packets. Once you understand packets (and the other information presented in this section), you can start to pull back the covers on internet performance numbers.

Sending one packet at a time is not terribly efficient. TCP has a concept called *Slow Start* to determine what the correct congestion window should be for the current connection. The design goal for Slow Start is to allow a new connection to feel out the state of a network and avoid making an already congested network worse. It allows the sender to send an additional unacknowledged packet for every acknowledgment it receives. This means that on a new connection after the first acknowledgment, it could send two packets, and when those two are acknowledged, it could send four, and so on. This geometric growth soon reaches an upper limit defined in the protocol, at which point the connection will enter what is called the *congestion avoidance phase*. See Figure 3-4.

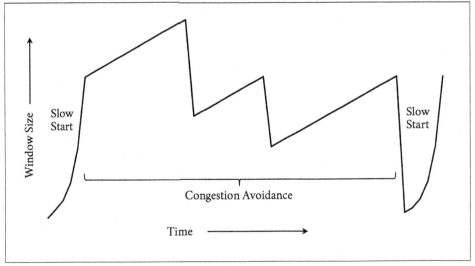

Figure 3-4. TCP congestion control (Reno algorithm)

It takes a few round-trips to get to the optimal congestion window size. And those few round-trips are precious time when it comes to addressing performance. Modern operating systems commonly use an initial congestion window size between 4 and 10 packets. When you consider a packet has a maximum size of around 1,460 bytes on the lower end, only 5,840 bytes can be sent before the sender needs to wait for acknowledgments. Today's web pages are averaging around 2 MB of data, including the HTML and all dependent objects. In a perfect world and with some generous hand waving, that means it will take around nine round-trips to transmit the page.

On top of that, since browsers are commonly opening six connections to a particular host, they need to do this for each connection.

Packet Math

Where did the preceding numbers come from? Understanding the math is an important tool for getting your head around estimating the effect of putting more or fewer bytes on the wire. Consider that the congestion window can double in size each round-trip and each packet can hold 1,460 bytes. In an idealized scenario you may envision something like the following table:

Round-trip	Packets sent	Max bytes sent	Total bytes sent
1	4	5840	5840
2	8	11680	17520
3	16	23360	40880
4	32	46720	87600
5	64	93440	181040
6	128	186880	367920
7	256	373760	741680
8	512	747520	1489200
9	1024	1495040	2984240

It is not until the ninth round-trip that 2 MB of data would have been sent. Unfortunately, this oversimplifies the real story. Well before a window size of 1024 would be reached, either a threshold called *ssthresh* would be hit or loss would occur, either of which would halt the geometric growth. This naive approach is sufficient, however, for the rough purposes we are using it for here.

Traditional TCP implementations employ congestion control algorithms that use loss as a feedback mechanism. When a packet is determined to have been lost, the algorithm will react by shrinking the congestion window. This is similar to navigating a dark room by deciding to turn when your shin collides with the coffee table. In the presence of timeouts where an expected response does not come in time, it will even reset the congestion window completely and reenter slow start. Newer algorithms take other factors into account, such as latency to provide a better feedback mechanism.

As previously mentioned, because h1 does not support multiplexing, a browser will commonly open up six connections to a particular host. This means this congestion window dance needs to occur six times in parallel. TCP will make certain that those connections play nicely together, but it does not guarantee that their performance will be optimal.

Fat message headers

Though h1 provides a mechanism for the compression of the requested objects, there is no way to compress the message headers. Headers can really add up, and though on responses the ratio of header size to object size may be very small, the headers make up the majority (if not all) of the bytes on requests. With cookies it is not uncommon for request headers to grow to a few kilobytes in size.

According to the HTTP archives, as of late 2016, the median request header is around 460 bytes. For a common web page with 140 objects on it, that means the total size of the requests is around 63 KB. Hark back to our discussion on TCP congestion window management and it might take three or four round-trips just to send the requests for the objects. The cost of the network latency begins to pile up quickly. Also, since upload bandwidth is often constrained by the network, especially in mobile cases, the windows might never get large enough to begin with, causing even more round-trips.

A lack of header compression can also cause clients to hit bandwidth limits. This is especially true on low-bandwidth or highly congested links. A classic example is the "Stadium Effect." When tens of thousands of people are in the same place at the same time (such as at a major sporting event), cellular bandwidth is quickly exhausted. Smaller requests with compressed headers would have an easier time in situations like that and put less overall load on the system.

Limited priorities

When a browser opens up multiple sockets (each of which suffers from head of line blocking) to a host and starts requesting objects, its options for indicating the priorities of those requests is limited: it either sends a request or not. Since some objects on a page are much more important than others, this forces even more serialization as the browser holds off on requesting objects to get the higher priority objects firsts. This can lead to having overall longer page downloads since the servers do not have the opportunity to work on the lower priority items as the browser potentially waits for processing on the higher priority items. It can also result in cases where a high-priority object is discovered, but due to how the browser processed the page it gets stuck behind lower priority items already being fetched.

Third-party objects

Though not specifically a problem with HTTP/1, we will round out the list with a growing performance issue. Much of what is requested on a modern web page is completely out of the control of the web server, what we refer to as *third-party* objects. Third-party object retrieval and processing commonly accounts for half of the time spent loading today's web pages. Though there are many tricks to minimize the impact of third-party objects on a page's performance, with that much content out of a web developer's direct control there is a good chance that some of those objects will have poor performance and delay or block the rendering of the page. Any discussion of web performance would be incomplete without mentioning this problem. (But, spoiler: h2 has no magic bullet with dealing with it either.)

What Do Third Parties Cost Me?

How much are third-party objects slowing down your page? Akamai's Foundry team has done a study that shows the effect can be quite dramatic, adding up to half of the total page load time in the median case.[1] This study proposes a new metric to track the effect of third parties called the *3rd Party Trailing Ratio*, which measures the percentage of page render time that is affected by the fetching and presentation of third-party content.

Web Performance Techniques

While working at Yahoo! in the early 2000s, Steve Souders and his team proposed and measured the impact of techniques aimed at making web pages load faster on client web browsers. This research led him to author two seminal books, *High Performance Websites*[2] and its follow-up *Even Faster Websites*,[3] which laid the ground work for the science of web performance.

Since then, more studies have confirmed the direct impact of performance on the website owner's bottom line, be it in terms of conversion rate, user engagement, or brand awareness. In 2010, Google added performance as one of the many parameters that come into play in its search engine to compute a given URL ranking.[4] As the importance of a web presence keeps growing for most businesses, it has become critical for organizations to understand, measure, and optimize website performance.

As discussed earlier in this chapter, for the majority of web pages the bulk of the browser's time is not spent serving the initial content (generally the HTML) from the

---

1 *http://akamai.me/2oEI9k9*

2 *http://oreil.ly/2pr0pQN*

3 *http://oreil.ly/2oni2ML*

4 *http://bit.ly/2pudXbs*

hosting infrastructure, but rather fetching all the assets and rendering the page on the client. This fact is captured by the diagram in Figure 3-5.[5]

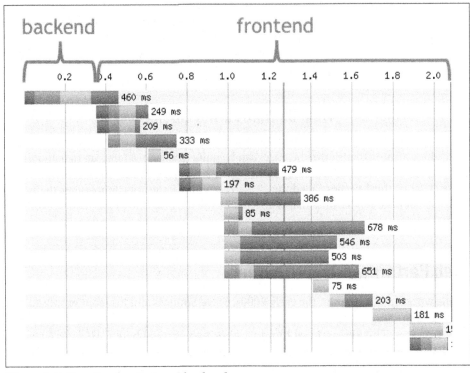

Figure 3-5. Timeline frontent and backend

As a result, there has been an increased emphasis among web developers on improving the performance by reducing the client's network latency and optimizing page render time. Quite literally, time is money.

Best Practices for Web Performance

As previously noted, the web has changed significantly—even in just the past few years. The relatively recent prevalence of mobile devices, the advances in JavaScript frameworks, and the evolution of the use of HTML warrant revisiting the rules laid out in the books referenced earlier, and going over the latest optimization techniques observed in the field.

---

5 *http://stevesouders.com/images/golden-waterfall.png*

Optimize DNS lookups

Since a DNS lookup needs to take place before a connection can be made to a host, it is critical that this resolution process be as fast as possible. The following best practices are a good place to start:

- Limit the number of unique domains/hostnames. Of course, this is not always in your control; however, the relative performance impact of the number of unique hostnames will only grow when moving to HTTP/2.
- Ensure low resolution latencies. Understand the topology of your DNS serving infrastructure and perform regular resolution time measurements from all the locations where your end users are (you can achieve this by using synthetic/real user monitoring). If you decide to rely on a third-party provider, select one best suited to your needs, as the quality of the services they offer can differ widely.
- Leverage DNS prefetch[6] from your initial HTML or response. This will start DNS resolution of specific hostnames on the page while the initial HTML is being downloaded and processed. For example, the following will prefetch a DNS resolution for ajax.googleapis.com:

```
<link rel="dns-prefetch" href="//ajax.googleapis.com">
```

These techniques will help ensure the fixed overhead of DNS is minimized.

Optimize TCP connections

As discussed earlier in this chapter, opening new connections can be a time-consuming process. If the connection uses TLS (as they all should), the overhead is even higher. Mitigations for this overhead include:

- Leverage preconnect,[7] as it will remove connection times from the waterfall critical path by having the connection established before it is needed. For example:

```
<link rel="preconnect" href="//fonts.example.com" crossorigin>
```

- Use early termination. Leveraging a Content Delivery Network (CDN), connections can be terminated at the edges of the internet located close to the requesting client, and therefore can greatly minimize the round-trip latencies incurred by establishing a new connection. See "Content Delivery Networks (CDNs)" on page 95 for more information on CDNs.

---

6 *https://www.w3.org/TR/resource-hints/#dns-prefetch*

7 *https://www.w3.org/TR/resource-hints/#preconnect*

- Implement the latest TLS best practices[8] for optimizing HTTPS.

If a lot of resources are requested from the same hostname, the client browsers will automatically open parallel connections to the server to avoid resource-fetching bottlenecks. You don't have direct control over the number of parallel connections a client browser will open for a given hostname, although most browsers now support six or more.

Avoid redirects

Redirects usually trigger connections to additional hostnames, which means an extra connection needs to be established. On radio networks (think mobile phones), an additional redirect may add hundreds of ms in latency, which is detrimental to the user experience, and eventually detrimental to the business running the websites. The obvious solution is to remove redirects entirely, as more often than not there is no "good" justification for some of them. If they cannot be simply removed, then you have two options:

- Leverage a CDN to perform the redirect "in the cloud" on behalf of the client
- If it is a same host redirect, use rewrite rules on the web server to avoid the redirect and map the user to the needed resource

Oftentimes, redirects are used to help with the dark art of Search Engine Optimization (SEO) to avoid short-term search result pain or consequent backend information layout changes. In such cases, you have to decide whether the redirect cost is worth the SEO benefits. Sometimes tearing the Band-Aid off in one go is the best long-term solution.

Cache on the client

Nothing is faster than retrieving an asset from the local cache, as no network connection is involved. As the saying goes (or at least will starting now), the fastest request is the one you do not make. In addition, when the content is retrieved locally, no charge is incurred either by the ISP or the CDN provider. The directive that tells the browser how long to cache an object is called the Time to Live, or TTL. Finding the best TTL for a given resource is not a perfect science; however, the following tried-and-tested guidelines are a good starting point:

- So-called truly static content, like images or versioned content, can be cached forever on the client. Keep in mind, though, that even if the TTL is set to expire in a long time, say one month away, the client may have to fetch it from the origin

---

8 *https://istlsfastyet.com/*

before it expires due to premature eviction or cache wipes. The actual TTL will eventually depend on the device characteristics (specifically the amount of available disk storage for the cache) and the end user's browsing habits and history.

- For CSS/JS and personalized objects, cache for about twice the median session time. This duration is long enough for most users to get the resources locally while navigating a website, and short enough to almost guarantee fresh content will be pulled from the network during the next navigation session.
- For other types of content, the ideal TTL will vary depending on the staleness threshold you are willing to live with for a given resource, so you'll have to use your best judgment based on your requirements.

Client caching TTL can be set through the HTTP header "cache control" and the key "max-age" (in seconds), or the "expires" header.

Cache at the edge

Caching at the edge of the network provides a faster user experience and can offload the serving infrastructure from a great deal of traffic as all users can benefit from the shared cache in the cloud.

A resource, to be cacheable, must be:

- Shareable between multiple users, and
- Able to accept some level of staleness

Unlike client caching, items like personal information (user preferences, financial information, etc.) should never be cached at the edge since they cannot be shared. Similarly, assets that are very time sensitive, like stock tickers in a real-time trading application, should not be cached. This being said, everything else is cacheable, even if it's only for a few seconds or minutes. For assets that don't change very frequently but must be updated on very short notice, like breaking news, for instance, leverage the purging mechanisms offered by all major CDN vendors. This pattern is called "Hold 'til Told": cache it forever until told not to.

Conditional caching

When the cache TTL expires, the client will initiate a request to the server. In many instances, though, the response will be identical to the cached copy and it would be a waste to re-download content that is already in cache. HTTP provides the ability to make conditional requests, which is effectively the client asking the server to, "Give me the object if it has changed, otherwise just tell me it is the same." Using conditional requests can have a significant bandwidth and performance savings when an object may not often change, but making the freshest version of the object available quickly is important. To use conditional caching:

- Include the Last-Modified-Since HTTP header in the request. The server will only return the full content if the latest content has been updated after the date in the header, else it will return a 304 response, with a new timestamp "Date" in the response header.

- Include an entity tag, or *ETag*, with the request that uniquely identifies the object. The ETag is provided by the server in a header along with the object itself. The server will compare the current ETag with the one received from the request header, and if they match will only return a 304, else the full content.

Most web servers will honor these techniques for images and CSS/JS, but you should check that it is also in place for any other cached content.

Compression and minification

All textual content (HTML, JS, CSS, SVG, XML, JSON, fonts, etc.), can benefit from compression and minification. These two methods can be combined to dramatically reduce the size of the objects. Fewer bytes means fewer round-trips, which means less time spent.

Minification is a process for sucking all of the nonessential elements out of a text object. Generally these objects are written by humans in a manner that makes them easy to read and maintain. The browser does not care about readability, however, and removing that *readability* can save space. As a trivial example, consider the following HTML:

```
<html>
<head>
  <!-- Change the title as you see fit -->
  <title>My first web page</title>
</head>
<body>
<!-- Put your message of the day here -->
<p>Hello, World!</p>
</body>
</html>
```

This is a perfectly acceptable HTML page and will render perfectly (if boringly) in a browser. But there is information in it that the browser does not need, including comments, newlines, and spaces. A minified version could look like:

```
<html><head><title>My first web page</title></head><body>
<p>Hello, World!</p></body></html>
```

It is not as pretty nor as maintainable, but it takes half the number of bytes (92 versus 186).

Compression adds another layer of savings on top of minification. Compression takes objects and reduces their size in an algorithmic way that can be reversed without loss.

A server will compress objects before they are sent and result in a 90% reduction in bytes on the wire. Common compression schemes include gzip and deflate, with a relative newcomer, Brotli, beginning to enter the scene.

Avoid blocking CSS/JS

CSS instructions will tell the client browser how and where to render content in the viewing area. As a consequence, clients will make sure to download all the CSS before painting the first pixel on the screen. While the browser pre-parser can be smart and fetch all the CSS it needs from the entire HTML early on, it is still a good practice to place all the CSS resource requests early in the HTML, in the head section of the document, and before any JS or images are fetched and processed.

JS will by default be fetched, parsed, and executed at the point it is located in the HTML, and will block the downloading and rendering of any resource past the said JS, until the browser is done with it. In some instances, it is desirable to have the downloading and execution of a given JS block the parsing and execution of the remainder of the HTML; for instance, when it instantiates a so-called tag-manager, or when it is critical that the JS be executed first to avoid references to nonexisting entities or race conditions.

However, most of the time this default blocking behavior incurs unnecessary delays and can even lead to single points of failure. To mitigate the potential negative effects of blocking JS, we recommend different strategies for both first-party content (that you control) and third-party content (that you don't control):

- Revisit their usage periodically. Over time, it is likely the web page keeps downloading some JS that may no longer be needed, and removing it is the fastest and most effective resolution path!

- If the JS execution order is not critical and it must be run before the onload event triggers, then set the "async"[9] attribute, as in:

  ```
  <script async src="/js/myfile.js">.
  ```

  This alone can improve your overall user experience tremendously by downloading the JS in parallel to the HTML parsing. Watch out for document.write directives as they would most likely break your pages, so test carefully!

- If the JS execution ordering is important and you can afford to run the scripts after the DOM is loaded, then use the "defer" attribute,[10] as in:

  ```
  <script defer src="/js/myjs.js">
  ```

---

9 *http://caniuse.com/#search=async*

10 *http://caniuse.com/#search=defer*

- If the JS is not critical to the initial view, then you should only fetch (and process) the JS after the onload event fires.

- You can consider fetching the JS through an iframe if you don't want to delay the main onload event, as it'll be processed separately from the main page. However, JS downloaded through an iframe may not have access to the main page elements.

If all this sounds a tad complicated, that's because it is. There is no one-size-fits-all solution to this problem, and it can be hazardous to recommend a particular strategy without knowing the business imperatives and the full HTML context. The preceding list, though, is a good starting point to ensure that no JS is left blocking the rendering of the page without a valid reason.

Optimize images

The relative and absolute weight of images for the most popular websites keeps increasing over time. The chart[11] in Figure 3-6 shows the number of requests and bytes size per page over a five-year period.

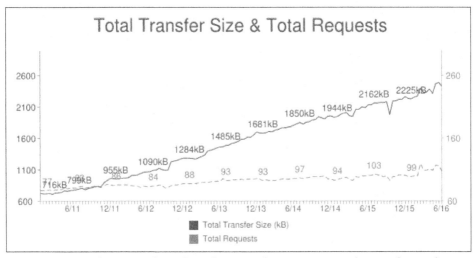

Figure 3-6. Transfer size and number of requests from 2011–2016 (source: httparchive.com)

Since most modern websites are dominated by images, optimizing them can yield some of the largest performance benefits. Image optimizations all aim at delivering the fewest bytes to achieve a given visual quality. Many factors negatively influence this goal and ought to be addressed:

---

11 *http://bit.ly/2pudJks*

- Image "metadata," like the subject location, timestamps, image dimension, and resolution are often captured with the binary information, and should be removed before serving to the clients (just ensure you don't remove the copyright and ICC profile data). This quality-lossless process can be done at build time. For PNG images, it is not unusual to see gains of about 10% in size reduction. If you want to learn more about image optimizations, you can read *High Performance Images* (O'Reilly 2016) by Tim Kadlec, Colin Bendell, Mike McCall, Yoav Weiss, Nick Doyle, and Guy Podjarny.

- Image overloading refers to images that end up being scaled down by the browsers, either because the natural dimensions exceed the placement size in the browser viewport, or because the image resolution exceeds the device display's capability. This scaling down not only wastes bandwidth, but also consumes significant CPU resources, which are sometimes in short supply for handheld devices. We commonly witness this effect in Responsive Web Design (RWD) sites, which indiscriminately serve the same images regardless of the rendering device. Figure 3-7 captures this over-download issue.

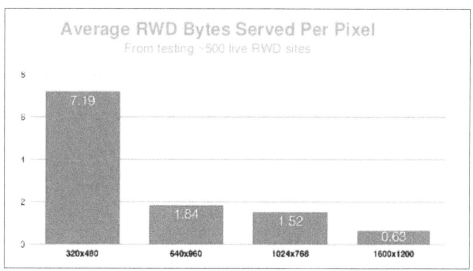

Figure 3-7. Average RWD bytes served per pixel. Source: http://goo.gl/6hOkQp

Techniques for mitigating image overloading involve serving images that are tailored (in terms of size and quality) to the user's device, network conditions, and the expected visual quality.

Anti-Patterns

Because HTTP/2 will only open a single connection per hostname, some HTTP/1.1 best practices are turning into anti-patterns for h2. The following sections discuss some popular methods that no longer apply to h2-enabled websites.

Spriting and resource consolidation/inlining

Spriting aims at consolidating many small images into a larger one in order to only incur one resource request for multiple image elements. For instance, color swatches or navigation elements (arrows, icons, etc.) get consolidated into one larger image, called a sprite. In the HTTP/2 model, where a given request is no longer blocking and many requests can be handled in parallel, spriting becomes moot from a performance standpoint and website administrators no longer need to worry about creating them, although it is probably not worth the effort to undo them.

In the same vein, small text-like resources like JS and CSS are routinely consolidated into single larger resources, or embedded into the main HMTL, so as to also reduce the number of client-server connections. One negative effect is that a small CSS or JS, which may be cacheable on its own, may become inherently uncacheable if embedded in an otherwise noncacheable HTML, so such practices should be avoided when a site migrates from h1 to h2. However, a study published by khanacademy.org,[12] November 2015, shows that packaging many small JS files into one may still make sense over h2, both for compression and CPU-saving purposes.

Sharding

Sharding aims at leveraging the browser's ability to open multiple connections per hostname to parallelize asset download. The optimum number of shards for a given website is not an exact science and it's fair to say that different views still prevail in the industry.

In an HTTP/2 world, it would require a significant amount of work for site administrators to unshard resources. A better approach is to keep the existing sharding, while ensuring the hostnames share a common certificate (Wildcard/SAN), mapped to the same server IP and port, in order to benefit from the browser network coalescence and save the connection establishment to each sharded hostname.

Cookie-less domains

In HTTP/1 the content of the request and response headers is never compressed. As the size of the headers has increased over time, it is no longer unusual to see cookie sizes larger than a single TCP packet (~1.5 KB). As a result, the cost of shuttling

---

12 *http://engineering.khanacademy.org/posts/js-packaging-http2.htm*

header information back and forth between the origin and the client may amount to measurable latency.

It was therefore a rational recommendation to set up cookie-less domains for resources that don't rely on cookies, for instance, images.

With HTTP/2 though, the headers are compressed (see "Header Compression (HPACK)" on page 56 in Chapter 5) and a "header history" is kept at both ends to avoid transmitting information already known. So if you perform a site redesign you can make your life simpler and avoid cookie-less domains.

Serving static objects from the same hostname as the HTML eliminates additional DNS lookups and (potentially) socket connections that delay fetching the static resources. You can improve performance by ensuring render-blocking resources are delivered over the same hostname as the HTML.

Summary

HTTP/1.1 has bred a messy if not exciting world of performance optimizations and best practices. The contortions that the industry has gone through to eek out performance have been extraordinary. One of the goals of HTTP/2 is to make many (though not all) of these techniques obsolete. Regardless, understanding them and the reasons they work will provide a deeper understanding of the web and how it works.

CHAPTER 4

Transition to HTTP/2

To be flip and mildly unhelpful, one could say that in order to support HTTP/2 all you need to do is upgrade to a web server that speaks h2, or use a Content Delivery Network (CDN) that will front your website and speak it for you. Though true, it is glossing over a host of subtleties that may not be obvious and could result in unexpected higher costs or suboptimal performance. Here are a handful of the items you should consider before turning HTTP/2 on for your website:

- Browser support for h2
- Potential move to serving over TLS (HTTPS)
- Tuning your website for h2 (possibly untuning for h1)
- Third parties on your site
- Retaining support for old clients

This chapter explains what you need to know about each of these topics.

Browser Support

As of publishing time, around 80% of web browsers in use support h2 to some degree.[1] This means a significant portion of people will start reaping the benefits of h2 as soon as it is turned on. Since the protocol negotiation is transparent to non-h2 supporting browsers, anyone who does not speak h2 will simply fall back to h1 and still access your infrastructure. (You did keep h1 support for now, right?)

Table 4-1 lists browsers and the latest version supporting HTTP/2.

---

1 *http://caniuse.com/#search=http2*

Table 4-1. HTTP/2 browser support

Name	Since version	Notes
Chrome	41	
Firefox	36	
Edge	12	
Safari	9	OSX 10.11 and later
Internet Explorer	11	Windows 10 only
Opera	28	
Safari - iOS	9.2	
Android Browser	51	
Chrome - Android	51	

Moving to TLS

Since all major browsers will only access h2 over TLS (i.e., an HTTPS request), that means you need to support TLS or you do not get to play. On top of that the TLS bar has been set quite high: you need to support at least TLS 1.2 with a specific set of ephemeral ciphers (see section 9.2 of RFC 7540 for details). Most modern security-conscious websites are already on the "TLS everywhere" bandwagon so it might just be a no-op for you, but if not, then there is an investment in time and resources to be made.

 This section is not intended to be a primer on securing your website with TLS. Whole books have been written on the subject. Managing your site's security is a tricky business with many traps for the unwary. Spend time to learn the tools your site depends on. For an excellent primer on TLS and certificates, check out Ilya Grigorik's book *High Performance Browser Networking*.

Much has been done over the past five years or so to make moving to and using TLS on your website as painless as possible, but it is still additional work. Items to consider are:

Understand your web server
Every web server has a slightly different way to configure its HTTPS settings.

Obtain a certificate
EV, OV, DV, CN, CSR, X509, SAN—there's a whole new alphabet soup of acronyms to wade through. Getting a certificate for your site generally involves a number of steps, including the creation of a Certificate Signing Request, verifying your identity and the ownership of the names the certificate is for, and purchasing the certificate from a Certificate Authority (CA). There are many CAs to

choose from. Organizations such as Let's Encrypt[2] are working to make it simple, fast, and even free to get a certificate.

Protect your private key

Your certificate is only as secure as you make it. To safely run a site over TLS, you need to consider how and where your private keys are stored and who has access to them. Solutions range from using very expensive Hardware Security Modules (HSMs) through finger crossing and good practices. If TLS is new to you, this will be an important aspect of your operational plan.

Prepare for increased server load

There has been a lot of effort to make TLS as inexpensive as possible, but it is a game of three steps forward and two back. Optimizations in symmetric ciphers have helped enormously, but moving to ephemeral key exchange has done the opposite (though it has made everything a lot more secure). Here are some best practices to get you started:

- Keep connections open as long as possible. The most expensive part of TLS is the handshake at connection time. If you keep the connection open for as long as possible, you will reduce the number of handshakes needed.

- Use session tickets. Session tickets allow a client to reconnect to the server, reusing the computationally expensive crypto work done in a previous handshake.

- Use a chipset with built-in crypto support. Intel's AES-NI[3] instructions in its modern processors make very quick work of symmetric cryptography.

Keep up with changes

Web security is a dynamic world. There is a new vulnerability in servers and HTTPS seemingly every couple of months. It is important to keep up with the "latest and greatest" to ensure your work of yesterday is not useless tomorrow.

Regularly check your site

You should use tools such as Qualys Lab's SSL Test[4] to check your site's TLS configuration.

---

2 *https://letsencrypt.org*

3 *http://intel.ly/2onh9E4*

4 *https://www.ssllabs.com/*

These best practices are good things to internalize for anyone standing up a service dependent on TLS, but TLS is a rich subject that requires a significant investment in time to fully appreciate. Remember:

A little learning is a dangerous thing; Drink deep, or taste not the Pierian spring.

—Alexander Pope

Is TLS Required?

The short answer is no. The useful answer is yes. Though HTTP/2 does not *require* TLS by specification, and in fact provides the ability to negotiate the protocol in the clear, no major browsers support h2 without TLS. There are two rationales behind this.

The wholly practical reason is that previous experiments with WebSocket and SPDY showed that using the Upgrade header and going over port 80 (the *in the clear* HTTP port) resulted in a very high error rate caused by things such as interrupting proxies. Putting the requests over TLS on port 443 (the HTTPS port) resulted in a significantly lower error rate and a cleaner protocol negotiation. The second reason stems from a growing belief that everything should be encrypted for the safety and privacy of all. HTTP/2 was seen as an opportunity to promote encrypted communications across the web going forward.

Undoing HTTP 1.1 "Optimizations"

Web developers have put a lot of effort into getting the most out of h1. Best practices have emerged such as concatenation, sharding, minification, cookieless domains, and spriting, to name a few. So you may be surprised to learn that some of these patterns become anti-patterns under h2. For example, concatenation (taking many CSS or JavaScript files and melding them into one) can potentially save a browser from making a bunch of requests. This was important with h1 where requests were expensive, but under h2 they are much more optimized. Skipping concatenation might mean very little request overhead and better fine-grained browser caching of the individual files.

Table 4-2 lists some common tricks used to optimize h1 requests, and notes considerations for h2.

Table 4-2. HTTP/1 optimizations, and related suggestions for HTTP/2

Name	Description	Notes
Concatenation	Combining multiple files (JavaScript, CSS) into one to reduce HTTP requests	This is less needed in HTTP/2 since the request overhead in bytes and time is much less, though not zero.
Minification	Taking unnecessary bytes out of files such as HTML, JavaScript, and CSS	A great thing to keep doing with HTTP/2.
Sharding	Spreading objects across multiple domains to get browsers to use more sockets	HTTP/2 is designed to use a single socket and using sharding would break that goal. Undo sharding, but see the note that follows this table, which explores the grayness of this topic.
Cookieless Domains	Having domains for things such as images use no cookies to minimize request sizes	Separate domains for objects should be avoided (see sharding), but more importantly, because of header compression in HTTP/2, the overhead of a cookie is significantly reduced.
Spriting	Making image maps of multiple images and using CSS to slice and dice them on a web page	This is similar to minification with the added aspect that the CSS work can get quite expensive. Deprecate this when using HTTP/2.

To Shard or Not to Shard?

HTTP/2 was designed to work optimally over a single TCP/IP socket. The idea is that getting one socket up and running at an optimal congestion rate was more reliable and performant than getting multiple sockets tuned in. However, research by Akamai's Foundry team indicates that this strategy is not a slam dunk.[5] Depending on the makeup of the site, we may still be in a world where multiple sockets will win over a single socket. This has everything to do with how TCP congestion control works and how long it takes to dial in the optimal settings. Starting with a significantly higher initial congestion window would help mitigate this problem, but larger windows can come with their own problems on networks that cannot support them. This is just one example that shows we as an industry are learning in real time about how to best use and optimize h2. When it comes to your site: develop, test, tweak, and repeat in order to find the optimal setup.

Assuming you take the time to fully optimize your site for h2, a problem immediately surfaces: you still have 25% of your traffic coming from h1 clients and you want to maximize their performance as well. Making everyone happy is an onerous task. Careful analysis of your users might tell you which group you should optimize for. Alternatively, you can conditionally serve different content for your h1 and h2 users, or use a CDN or similar tool that can do the magic for you.[6]

---

5 *http://akamai.me/2oEPSOZ*

6 *http://akamai.me/2onjVcz*

Third Parties

We love them and hate them, but third-party content on our sites is a reality. The problem with third-party content is you do not directly control it and are therefore at the mercy of what those third parties do and do not support. If h2 works best when everything is on a single socket, where do third parties come in? Being realistic, they do not, and they can become a major drag on any potential performance gain you might see from HTTP/2. The headache becomes even bigger if the third parties you use do not have a TLS option. Research[7] into the effect of third-party content on page performance has determined that, in many cases, it is one of the largest factors in a page's performance.

So what to do about third-party content? Start by finding out the answers to the following questions:

- Does your third party have a TLS option?
- Do they have plans to support HTTP/2?
- Do they see minimizing performance impact as a critical element of what they provide?

If the answer to any of these questions is "no," then there are two follow-up questions: "Are there other third parties that provide what I need?" and "Do I really need this third-party content, or could I live without?"

Supporting Older Clients

Some people do not like change. Their current browser works for them, and upgrading can be a nuisance. The problem is that these people may be your customers or users and you may not be ready to abandon them. Here is a real example. Microsoft ended support of Windows XP on April 8, 2014. This means that users on XP are falling farther and farther behind in terms of modern browsers and security. Needless to say, Internet Explorer on XP cannot talk h2, but more importantly, depending on how your TLS settings are configured and whether you have a clear-text fallback site, those users might not be able to even access your site over h1! On one hand this is the inevitability of progress, but on the other hand these could be important users and customers for you. This reality is yet one more item to consider before making the move to HTTP/2.

---

7 *http://akamai.me/2oEI9k9*

Summary

Though a transition to HTTP/2 is generally seen as a good thing and should be completely transparent to your website, there are certainly considerations that you need to take into account before flipping the switch. Even though many major websites have been running h2 for some time now, that does not mean it is a guaranteed win for your situation. It should be treated the same as any other significant change: test, test, test.

CHAPTER 5

The HTTP/2 Protocol

This chapter provides an overview of how HTTP/2 works at a low level, down to the frames on the wire and how they interact. It will help you understand many of the benefits (and problems) the protocol provides. By the end you should have enough information to get started with tuning and debugging your own h2 installations in order to get the most out of the protocol. For the brave who would like to go deeper into the protocol, perhaps for implementation purposes, RFC 7540[1] is an excellent place to start.

Layers of HTTP/2

HTTP/2 can be generalized into two parts: the *framing layer*, which is core to h2's ability to multiplex, and the *data* or *http* layer, which contains the portion that is traditionally thought of as HTTP and its associated data. It is tempting to completely separate the two layers and think of them as totally independent things. Careful readers of the specification will note that there is a tension between the framing layer being a completely generic reusable construct, and being something that was designed to transport HTTP. For example, the specification starts out talking generically about endpoints and bidirectionality—something that would be perfect for many messaging applications—and then segues into talking about clients, servers, requests, and responses. When reading about the framing layer it is important to not lose sight of the fact that its purpose is to transport and communicate HTTP and nothing else.

---

1 *https://tools.ietf.org/html/rfc7540*

Though the data layer is purposely designed to be backward compatible with HTTP/1.1, there are a number of aspects of h2 that will cause developers familiar with h1 and accustomed to reading the protocol on the wire to perform a double take:

Binary protocol
> The h2 framing layer is a binary framed protocol. This makes for easy parsing by machines but causes eye strain when read by humans.

Header compression
> As if a binary protocol were not enough, in h2 the headers are heavily compressed. This can have a dramatic effect on redundant bytes on the wire.

Multiplexed
> When looking at a connection that is transporting h2 in your favorite debugging tool, requests and responses will be interwoven with each other.

Encrypted
> To top it off, for the most part the data on the wire is encrypted, making reading on the fly more challenging.

We will explore each of these topics in the ensuing pages.

The Connection

The base element of any HTTP/2 session is the connection. This is defined as a TCP/IP socket initiated by the client, the entity that will send the HTTP requests. This is no different than h1; however, unlike h1, which is completely stateless, h2 bundles connection-level elements that all of the frames and streams that run over it adhere to. These include connection-level settings and the header table (which are both described in more detail later in this chapter). This implies a certain amount of overhead in each h2 connection that does not exist in earlier versions of the protocol. The intent is that the benefits of that overhead far outweigh the costs.

Sprechen Sie h2?

Protocol discovery—knowing that an endpoint can support the protocol you want to speak—can be tricky business. HTTP/2 provides two mechanisms to discovery.

In cases where the connection is not encrypted, the client will leverage the Upgrade header to indicate a desire to speak h2. If the server can speak h2, it replies with a "101 Switching Protocols" response. This adds a full round-trip to the communication.

If the connection is over TLS, however, the client sets the Application-Layer Protocol Negotiation (ALPN) extension in the ClientHello to indicate the desire to speak h2 and the server replies in kind. In this way h2 is negotiated *in line* with no additional

---

round-trips. It is worth noting that SPDY and early revisions of h2 used the Next Protocol Negotiation (NPN) extension to negotiate h2. This was dropped in favor of ALPN in mid-2014.

One last way to indicate support for h2 is to use HTTP Alternative Services[2] or *Alt-Svc*. This provides the server a method for indicating in a response header to the client that there may be a better location or protocol to use for future requests. It is a highly flexible tool with growing browser support. It is not intended to be a replacement for ALPN, but it is a powerful tool to be aware of.

In order to doubly confirm to the server that the client endpoint speaks h2, the client sends a magic octet stream called the connection preface as the first data over the connection. This is primarily intended for the case where a client has upgraded from HTTP/1.1 over clear text. This stream in hex is:

```
0x505249202a20485454502f322e300d0a0d0a534d0d0a0d0a
```

Decoded as ASCII you get:

```
PRI * HTTP/2.0\r\n\r\nSM\r\n\r\n
```

The point of this string is to cause an explicit error if by some chance the server (or some intermediary) did not end up being able to speak h2. The message is purposely formed to look like an h1 message. If a well-behaving h1 server receives this string, it will choke on the method (PRI) or the version (HTTP/2.0) and will return an error, allowing the h2 client to explicitly know something bad happened.

This magic string is then followed immediately by a SETTINGS frame. The server, to confirm its ability to speak h2, acknowledges the client's SETTINGS frame and replies with a SETTINGS frame of its own (which is in turn acknowledged) and the world is considered good and h2 can start happening. Much work went into making certain this dance was as efficient as possible. Though it may seem on the surface that this is worryingly chatty, the client is allowed to start sending frames right away, assuming that the server's SETTINGS frame is coming. If by chance the overly optimistic client receives something before the SETTINGS frame, the negotiation has failed and everyone gets to GOAWAY.

---

2 *https://tools.ietf.org/html/rfc7838*

Frames

As mentioned before, HTTP/2 is a framed protocol. Framing is a method for wrapping all the important stuff in a way that makes it easy for consumers of the protocol to read, parse, and create. In contrast, h1 is not framed but is rather text delimited. Look at the following simple example:

```
GET / HTTP/1.1 <crlf>
Host: www.example.com <crlf>
Connection: keep-alive <crlf>
Accept: text/html,application/xhtml+xml,application/xml;q=0.9... <crlf>
User-Agent: Mozilla/5.0 (Macintosh; Intel Mac OS X 10_11_4)... <crlf>
Accept-Encoding: gzip, deflate, sdch <crlf>
Accept-Language: en-US,en;q=0.8 <crlf>
Cookie: pfy_cbc_lb=p-browse-w; customerZipCode=99912|N; ltc=%20;... <crlf>
<crlf>
```

Parsing something like this is not rocket science but it tends to be slow and error prone. You need to keep reading bytes until you get to a delimiter, <crlf> in this case, while also accounting for all of the less spec-compliant clients that just send <lf>. A state machine looks something like this:

```
loop
while( ! CRLF )
 read bytes
end while

if first line
  parse line as the Request-Line
else if line is empty
  break out of the loop # We are done
else if line starts with non-whitespace
  parse the header line into a key/value pair
else if line starts with space
```

```
  add the continuation header to the previous header
 end if
end loop

# Now go on to ready the request/response based on whatever was
# in the Transfer-encoding header and deal with all of the vagaries
# of browser bugs
```

Writing this code is very doable and has been done countless times. The problems with parsing an h1 request/response are:

- You can only have one request/response on the wire at a time. You have to parse until done.

- It is unclear how much memory the parsing will take. This leads to a host of questions: What buffer are you reading a line into? What happens if that line is too long? Should you grow and reallocate, or perhaps return a 400 error? These types of questions makes working in a memory efficient and fast manner challenging.

Frames, on the other hand, let the consumer know up front what they will be getting. Framed protocols in general, and h2 specifically, start with some known number of bytes that contain a length field for the overall size of the frame. Figure 5-1 shows what an HTTP/2 frame looks like.

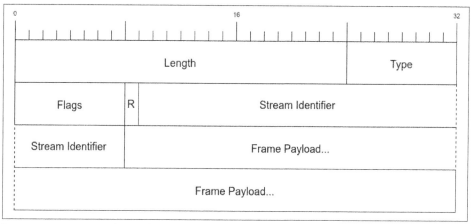

Figure 5-1. HTTP/2 frame header

The first nine bytes (octets) are consistent for every frame. The consumer just needs to read those bytes and it knows precisely how many bytes to expect in the whole frame. See Table 5-1 for a description of each field.

Table 5-1. HTTP/2 frame header fields

Name	Length	Description
Length	3 bytes	Indicates the length of the frame payload (value in the range of 2^{14} through 2^{24-1} bytes). Note that 2^{14} bytes is the default max frame size, and longer sizes must be requested in a SETTINGS frame.
Type	1 bytes	What type of frame this is (see Table 5-2 for a description).
Flags	1 bytes	Flags specific to the frame type.
R	1 bit	A reserved bit. Do not set this. Doing so might have dire consequences.
Stream Identifier	31 bits	A unique identifier for each stream.
Frame Payload	Variable	The actual frame content. Its length is indicated in the Length field.

Because everything is deterministic, the parsing logic is more like:

```
loop
  Read 9 bytes off the wire
  Length = the first three bytes
  Read the payload based on the length.
  Take the appropriate action based on the frame type.
end loop
```

This is much simpler to write and maintain. It also has a second extremely significant advantage over h1's delimited format: with h1 you need to send a complete request or response before you can send another. Because of h2's framing, requests and responses can be interwoven, or multiplexed. Multiplexing helps get around problems such as head of line blocking, which was described in "Head of line blocking" on page 17.

There are 10 different frame types in the protocol. Table 5-2 provides a brief description, and you are welcome to jump to Appendix A if you'd like to learn more about each one.

Table 5-2. HTTP/2 frame types

Name	ID	Description
DATA	0x0	Carries the core content for a stream
HEADERS	0x1	Contains the HTTP headers and, optionally, priorities
PRIORITY	0x2	Indicates or changes the stream priority and dependencies
RST_STREAM	0x3	Allows an endpoint to end a stream (generally an error case)
SETTINGS	0x4	Communicates connection-level parameters
PUSH_PROMISE	0x5	Indicates to a client that a server is about to send something
PING	0x6	Tests connectivity and measures round-trip time (RTT)
GOAWAY	0x7	Tells an endpoint that the peer is done accepting new streams
WINDOW_UPDATE	0x8	Communicates how many bytes an endpoint is willing to receive (used for flow control)
CONTINUATION	0x9	Used to extend HEADER blocks

Room for Extension

HTTP/2 built in the ability to handle new frame types called *extension* frames. This provides a mechanism for client and server implementors to experiment with new frame types without having to create a whole new protocol. Since by specification any frame that is not understood by a consumer must be discarded, new frames on the wire should not affect the core protocol. Of course, if your application is reliant on a new frame and a proxy in the middle is dropping that frame, then you might run into a few problems.

Streams

The HTTP/2 specification defines a stream as "an independent, bidirectional sequence of frames exchanged between the client and server within an HTTP/2 connection." You can think of a stream as a series of frames making up an individual HTTP request/response pair on a connection. When a client wants to make a request it initiates a new stream. The server will then reply on that same stream. This is similar to the request/response flow of h1 with the important difference that because of the framing, multiple requests and responses can interleave together without one blocking another. The Stream Identifier (bytes 6–9 of the frame header) is what indicates which stream a frame belongs to.

After a client has established an h2 connection to the server, it starts a new stream by sending a HEADERS frame and potentially CONTINUATION frames if the headers need to span multiple frames (see "CONTINUATION Frames" on page 48 for more on the CONTINUATIONS frame). This HEADERS frame generally contains the

HTTP request or response, depending on the sender. Subsequent streams are initiated by sending a new HEADERS frame with an incremented Stream Identifier.

CONTINUATION Frames

HEADERS frames indicate that there are no more headers by setting the END_HEADERS bit in the frame's Flags field. In cases where the HTTP headers do not fit in a single HEADERS frame (e.g., the frame would be longer than the current max frame size) the END_HEADERS flag is not set and it is followed by one or more CONTINUATION frames. Think of the CONTINUATION frame as a special-case HEADERS frame. Why use a special frame and not just use a HEADERS frame again? Reusing HEADERS would necessitate doing something reasonable with the subsequent HEADERS Frame Payload. Should the frame headers be duplicated? If so, what happens if there is a disagreement between the frames? Protocol developers do not like vague cases like this as it can be a future source of problems. With that in mind, the working group's decision was to add a frame type that was explicit in its purpose to avoid implementation confusion.

It should be noted that because of the requirements that HEADERS and CONTINUATION frames must be sequential, using a CONTINUATION frames breaks or at least diminishes the benefits of multiplexing. CONTINUATION frames are a tool for addressing an important use case (large headers), but should only be used when necessary.

Messages

An HTTP message is a generic term for an HTTP request or response. As mentioned in the previous section, a stream is created to transport a pair of request/response messages. At a minimum a message consists of a HEADERS frame (which initiates the stream) and can additionally contain CONTINUATION and DATA frames, as well as additional HEADERS frames. Figure 5-2 is an example flow for a common GET request.

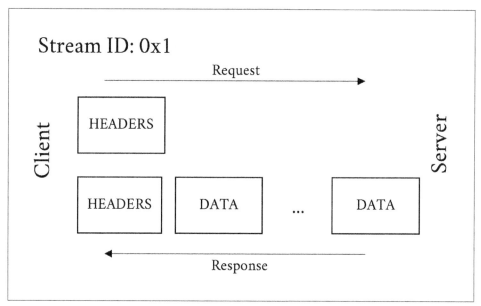

Figure 5-2. GET Request message and response message

And Figure 5-3 illustrates what the frames may look like for a POST message. Remember that the big difference between a POST and a GET is that a POST commonly includes data sent from the client.

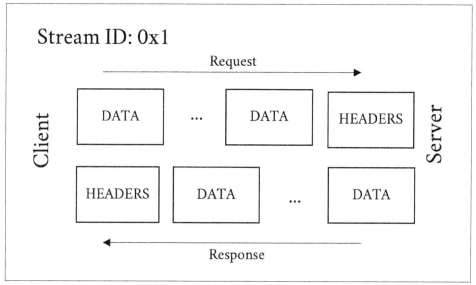

Figure 5-3. POST request message and response message

Just like h1 requests/responses are split into the message headers and the message body, an h2 request/response is split into HEADERS and DATA frames.

For reference, HTTP messages are defined in HTTP/1.1's RFC 7230.[3]

Here are a few notable difference between HTTP/1 and HTTP/2 messages:

Everything is a header
> h1 split messages into request/status lines and headers. h2 did away with this distinction and rolled those lines into magic *pseudo* headers. For example, a sample request and response in HTTP/1.1 might look like:

```
GET / HTTP/1.1
Host: www.example.com
User-agent: Next-Great-h2-browser-1.0.0
Accept-Encoding: compress, gzip

HTTP/1.1 200 OK
Content-type: text/plain
Content-length: 2
...
```

> And its HTTP/2 equivalent:

```
:scheme: https
:method: GET
:path: /
:authority: www.example.com
User-agent: Next-Great-h2-browser-1.0.0
Accept-Encoding: compress, gzip

:status: 200
content-type: text/plain
```

> Note how the request and status lines are split out into the :scheme, :method, :path, and :status headers. Also note that this representation of the h2 headers is not what goes over the wire. Skip to "HEADERS Frame Fields" on page 123 for a description of the HEADERS frame and "Header Compression (HPACK)" on page 56 for more on that.

No chunked encoding
> Who needs chunking in the world of frames? Chunking was used to piece out data to the peer without knowing the length ahead of time. With frames as part of the core protocol there is no need for it any longer.

---

3 *https://tools.ietf.org/html/rfc7230*

No more 101 responses

The Switching Protocols response is a corner case of h1. Its most common use today is probably for upgrading to a WebSocket connection. ALPN provides more explicit protocol negotiation paths with less round-trip overhead.

Flow Control

A new feature in h2 is stream flow control. Unlike h1 where the server will send data just about as fast as the client will consume it, h2 provides the ability for the client to pace the delivery. (And, as just about everything in h2 is symmetrical, the server can do the same thing.) Flow control information is indicated in WINDOW_UPDATE frames. Each frame tells the peer endpoint how many bytes the sender is willing to receive. As the endpoint receives and consumes sent data, it will send out a WINDOWS_UPDATE frame to indicate its updated ability to consume bytes. (Many an early HTTP/2 implementor spent a good deal of time debugging window updates to answer the "Why am I not getting data?" question.) It is the responsibility of the sender to honor these limits.

A client may want to use flow control for a variety of reasons. One very practical reason may be to make certain one stream does not choke out others. Or a client may have limited bandwidth or memory available and forcing the data to come down in manageable chunks will lead to efficiency gains. Though flow control cannot be turned off, setting the maximum value of 2^{31-1} effectively disables it, at least for files under 2 GB in size. Another case to keep in mind is intermediaries. Very often content is delivered through a proxy or CDN that terminated the HTTP connections. Because the different sides of the proxy could have different throughput capabilities, flow control allows a proxy to keep the two sides closely in sync to minimize the need for overly taxing proxy resources.

Flow Control Example

At the start of every stream, the window defaults to 65,535 ($2^{16}-1$) bytes. Assume a client endpoint A sticks with that default and its peer, B, sends 10,000 bytes. B keeps track of the window (now 55,535 bytes). Now, say A takes its time and consumes 5,000 bytes and sends out a WINDOW_UPDATE frame indicating that its window is now 60,535 bytes. B gets this and starts to send a large file (say, 4 GB). B can only send up to the current window size, 60,535 in this case, before it needs to wait for A to indicate that it is ready to receive more bytes. In this way, A can control the maximum rate B can send it data.

Priority

The last important characteristic of streams is dependencies. Modern browsers are very careful to ask for the most important elements on a web page first, which improves performance by fetching objects in an optimal order. Once it has the HTML in hand, the browser generally needs things like cascading style sheets (CSS) and critical JavaScript before it can start painting the screen. Without multiplexing, it needs to wait for a response to complete before it can ask for a new object. With h2, the client can send all of its requests for resources at the same time and a server can start working on those requests right away. The problem with that is the browser loses the implicit priority scheme that it had in h1. If the server receives a hundred requests for objects at the same time, with no indication of what is more important, it will send everything more or less simultaneously and the less important elements will get in the way of the critical elements.

HTTP/2 addresses this through stream dependencies. Using HEADERS and PRIORITY frames, the client can clearly communicate what it needs and the suggested order in which they are needed. It does this by declaring a *dependency* tree and the relative *weights* inside that tree:

- *Dependencies* provide a way for the client to tell the server that the delivery of a particular object (or objects) should be prioritized by indicating that other objects are dependent on it.
- *Weights* let the client tell the server how to prioritize objects that have a common dependency.

Take this simple website as an example:

- *index.html*
  - *header.jpg*
  - *critical.js*
  - *less_critical.js*
  - *style.css*
  - *ad.js*
  - *photo.jpg*

After receiving the base HTML file, the client could parse it and create a dependency tree, and assign weights to the elements in the tree. In this case the tree might look like:

- *index.html*
  - *style.css*
    - *critical.js*
      - *less_critical.js* (weight 20)
      - *photo.jpg* (weight 8)
      - *header.jpg* (weight 8)
      - *ad.js* (weight 4)

In this dependency tree, the client is communicating that it wants *style.css* before anything else, then *critical.js*. Without these two files, it can't make any forward progress toward rendering the web page. Once it has *critical.js*, it provides the relative weights to give the remaining objects. The weights indicate the relative amount of "effort" that should be expended serving an object. In this case *less_critical.js* has a weight of 20 relative to a total of 40 for all weights. This means the server should spend about half of its time and/or resources working on delivering *less_critical.js* compared to the other three objects. A well-behaved server will do what it can to make certain the client gets those objects as quickly as possible. In the end, what to do and how to honor priorities is up to the server. It retains the ability to do what it thinks is best. Intelligently dealing with priorities will likely be a major distinguishing performance factor between h2-capable web servers.

Server Push

The best way to improve performance for a particular object is to have it positioned in the browser's cache before it is even asked for. This is the goal of HTTP/2's Server Push feature. Push gives the server the ability to send an object to a client proactively, presumably because it knows that it will be needed at a near future date. Allowing a server to arbitrarily send objects down to a client could cause problems, including performance and security issues, so it is not just a matter of doing it, but also a matter of doing it well.

Pushing an Object

When the server decides it wants to push an object (referred to as "pushing a response" in the RFC), it constructs a PUSH_PROMISE frame. There are a number of important attributes to this frame:

- The stream ID in the PUSH_PROMISE frame header is the stream ID of the request that the response is associated with. A pushed response is always related to a request the client has already sent. For example, if a browser asks for a base

HTML page, a server would construct a PUSH_PROMISE on that request's stream ID for a JavaScript object on that page.

- The PUSH_PROMISE frame has a header block that resembles what the client would send if it were to request the object itself. This gives the client a chance to sanity check what is about to be sent.

- The object that is being sent must be considered cacheable.

- The :method header field must be considered safe. Safe methods are those that are *idempotent*, which is a fancy way of saying ones that do not change any state. For example, a GET request is considered idempotent as it is (usually) just fetching an object, while a POST request is considered nonidempotent because it may change state on the server side.

- Ideally the PUSH_PROMISE should be sent down to the client before the client receives the DATA frames that might refer to the pushed object. If the server were to send the full HTML down before the PUSH_PROMISE is sent, for example, the client might have already sent a request for the object before the PUSH_PROMISE is received. The h2 protocol is robust enough to deal with this situation gracefully, but there is wasted effort and opportunity.

- The PUSH_PROMISE frame will indicate what Stream Identifier the future sent response will be on.

 When a client chooses Stream Identifiers, it starts with 1 and then increments by two for each new stream, thus using only odd numbers. When a server initiates a new stream indicated in a PUSH_PROMISE it starts with 2 and sticks to even numbers. This avoids a race condition between the client and server on stream IDs and makes it easy to tell what objects were pushed. Stream 0 is reserved for overall connection-level control messages and cannot be used for new streams.

If a client is unsatisfied with any of the preceding elements of a PUSH_PROMISE, it can reset the new stream (with an RST_STREAM) or send a PROTOCOL_ERROR (in a GOAWAY frame), depending on the reason for the refusal. A common case could be that it already has the object in cache. The error responses are reserved for protocol-level problems with the PUSH_PROMISE such as unsafe methods or sending a push when the client has indicated that it would not accept push in a SETTINGS frame. It is worth noting that the server can start the stream right after the promise is sent, so canceling an in-flight push still may result in a good deal of the resource being sent. Pushing the right things and only the right things is an important performance feature.

Assuming the client does not refuse the push, the server will go ahead and send the object on the new stream identifier indicated in the PUSH_PROMISE (Figure 5-4).

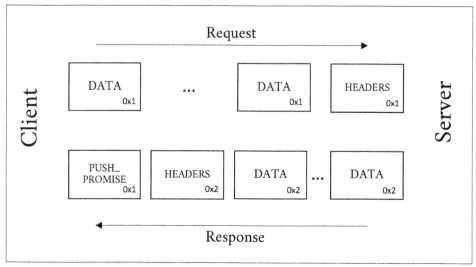

Figure 5-4. Server Push message processing

Choosing What to Push

Depending on the application, deciding what to push may be trivial or extraordinarily complex. Take a simple HTML page, for example. When a server gets a request for the page, it needs to decide if it is going to push the objects on that page or wait for the client to ask for them. The decision-making process should take into account:

- The odds of the object already being in the browser's cache
- The assumed priority of the object from the client's point of view (see "Priority" on page 52)
- The available bandwidth and similar resources that might have an effect on the client's ability to receive a push

If the server chooses correctly it can really help the performance of the overall page, but a poor decision can have the opposite effect. This is probably why general-purpose push solutions are relatively uncommon today, even though SPDY introduced the feature over five years ago.

A more specialized case such as an API or an application communicating over h2 might have a much easier time deciding what will be needed in the very near future and what the client does not have cached. Think of a server streaming updates to a native application. These are areas that will see the most benefit from push in the near term.

Header Compression (HPACK)

As mentioned in "Fat message headers" on page 20, the average web page requires around 140 requests and the median size of an HTTP request is 460 bytes, totaling 63 KB of requests. That can cause quite the delay in the best of circumstances, but when you think about a congested WiFi or a poor cellular connection, things can get downright painful. The real crime is that between those requests there are generally very few new and unique bytes. They are screaming out for some type of compression.

It was known from the start that header compression would be a key element of HTTP/2. But how should they be compressed? The browser world was just recovering from from the CRIME vulnerability in SPDY, which leveraged the deflate header compression in a creative way to decrypt the early encrypted frames, so that approach was out. There was a need for a CRIME-proof mechanism that would have similar compression ability as GZIP.

After much innovative deliberation, HPACK was proposed. HPACK is a table lookup compression scheme that leverages Huffman encoding to get compression rates that approach GZIP. The best way to understand how HPACK works is probably with a simplified example.

 Why not just use GZIP for header compression instead of HPACK? It would be a lot less work, for certain. Unfortunately the CRIME attack showed that it would also be vulnerable leakage of encrypted information. CRIME works by the attackers adding data to a request and then observing whether the resultant compressed and encrypted payload is smaller. If it is smaller they know that their inserted text overlaps with something else in the request such as a secret session cookie. In a relatively small amount of time the entire secret payload can be extracted in this manner. Thus, off-the-shelf compression schemes were out, and HPACK was invented.

Downloading a web page and its dependent objects involves many requests. This number commonly reaches into the hundreds for a single web page. These requests tend to be extremely similar. Take, for example, the following two requests. They are two requests that are likely to follow one another in a browser session requesting a full web page. The few unique bytes are emphasized in bold.

Request #1:

```
:authority: www.akamai.com
:method: GET
:path: /
:scheme: https
accept: text/html,application/xhtml+xml
accept-language: en-US,en;q=0.8
```

```
cookie: last_page=286A7F3DE
upgrade-insecure-requests: 1
user-agent: Awesome H2/1.0
```

Request #2:

```
:authority: www.akamai.com
:method: GET
:path: /style.css
:scheme: https
accept: text/html,application/xhtml+xml
accept-language: en-US,en;q=0.8
cookie: last_page=*398AB8E8F
upgrade-insecure-requests: 1
user-agent: Awesome H2/1.0
```

You can see that much of the latter request is a repeat of the former. The first request is about 220 bytes, and the second about 230. But only 36 bytes are unique. Just sending those 36 bytes will mean roughly an 85% savings in bytes sent. At a high level that is how HPACK works.

The following is a contrived and simplified example to help explain what HPACK is doing. The reality is much more of a stark, dystopian landscape, and if you're curious to learn more, you should read RFC 7541, "HPACK: Header Compression for HTTP/2."[4]

Let's assume a client sends the following headers, in order:

```
Header1: foo
Header2: bar
Header3: bat
```

When the client sends the request, it can indicate in the header block that a particular header and its value should be indexed. It would create a table like:

Index	Name	Value
62	Header1	foo
63	Header2	bar
64	Header3	bat

On the server side, when it reads the headers it would create the same table. On the next request when the client sends the request, if it sends the same headers it can simply send a header block like:

```
62 63 64
```

---

4 *https://tools.ietf.org/html/rfc7541*

which the server will then look up and expand into the full headers that those indexes represent.

One of the major implications of this is that each connection is maintaining state, something that was nonexistent at the protocol level for h1.

The reality of HPACK is much more complicated. Here are a few tidbits for the curious:

- There are actually two tables maintained on each side of a request or response. One is a dynamic table created in a manner similar to the preceding example. One is a static table made up of the 61 most common header names and value combinations. For example, :method: GET is in the static table at index 2. The static table is defined to be 61 entries long, hence why the example started at 62.
- There are a number of controls on how items are indexed. These include:
  — Send literal values and indexes (as in the preceding example)
  — Send literal values and do not index them (for one-off or sensitive headers)
  — Send an indexed header name with a literal value and do not index it (for things like :path: /foo.html where the value is always changing)
  — Send an indexed header and value (as in the second request of the previous example)
- It uses integer compression with a packing scheme for extreme space efficiency.
- Leverages Huffman coding table for further compression of string literals.

Experiments show that HPACK works very well, especially on sites with large repeated headers (think: cookies). Since the bulk of the headers that are sent from request to request to a particular website are duplicated, HPACK's table lookup mechanisms effectively eliminate those duplicate bytes from the communication.

On the Wire

Let's look at an hHTTP/2 request and response and break it down. Note again, though we are spelling them out in text here for easy visual consumption, h2 on the wire is in a binary format and is compressed.

A Simple GET

The GET is the workhorse of HTTP. Semantically simple, it does what it says. It gets a resource from a server. Take, for instance, Example 5-1, a request to akamai.com (lines are truncated for clarity).

Example 5-1. HTTP/2 GET request

```
:authority: www.akamai.com
:method: GET
:path: /
:scheme: https
accept: text/html,application/xhtml+xml,...
accept-language: en-US,en;q=0.8
cookie: sidebar_collapsed=0; _mkto_trk=...
upgrade-insecure-requests: 1
user-agent: Mozilla/5.0 (Macintosh;...
```

This request asks for the index page from www.akamai.com over HTTPS using the GET method. Example 5-2 shows the response.

 The :authority header's name may seem odd. Why not :host? The reason for this is that it is analogous to the Authority section of the URI and not the HTTP/1.1 Host header. The Authority section includes the host and optionally the port, and thus fills the role of the Host header quite nicely. For the few of you who jumped to and read the URI RFC,[5] the User Information section of the Authority (i.e., the username and password) is explicitly forbidden in h2.

Example 5-2. HTTP/2 GET response (headers only)

```
:status: 200
cache-control: max-age=600
content-encoding: gzip
content-type: text/html;charset=UTF-8
date: Tue, 31 May 2016 23:38:47 GMT
etag: "08c024491eb772547850bf157abb6c430-gzip"
expires: Tue, 31 May 2016 23:48:47 GMT
link: <https://c.go-mpulse.net>;rel=preconnect
set-cookie: ak_bmsc=8DEA673F92AC...
vary: Accept-Encoding, User-Agent
x-akamai-transformed: 9c 237807 0 pmb=mRUM,1
x-frame-options: SAMEORIGIN

<DATA Frames follow here>
```

In this response the server is saying that the request was successful (200 status code), sets a cookie (cookie header), indicates that the content is gzipped (content-encoding header), as well as a host of other important bits of information used behind the scenes.

---

5 *https://www.ietf.org/rfc/rfc3986.txt*

Now let's take our first look at what goes over the wire for a simple GET. Using Tatsu-hiro Tsujikawa's excellent nghttp tool,[6] we can get a verbose output to see all the living details of h2:

```
$ nghttp -v -n --no-dep -w 14 -a -H "Header1: Foo" https://www.akamai.com
```

This command line sets the window size to 16 KB (2^{14}), adds an arbitrary header, and asks to download a few key assets from the page. The following section shows the annotated output of this command:

```
[  0.047] Connected
The negotiated protocol: h2 ❶
[  0.164] send SETTINGS frame <length=12, flags=0x00, stream_id=0> ❷
         (niv=2)
         [SETTINGS_MAX_CONCURRENT_STREAMS(0x03):100]
         [SETTINGS_INITIAL_WINDOW_SIZE(0x04):16383]  ❸
```

Here you see that nghttp:

❶ Successfully negotiated h2

❷ As per spec, sent a SETTINGS frame right away

❸ Set the window size to 16 KB as requested in the command line

Note the use of stream_id 0 for the connection-level information. (You do not see the connection preface in the output but it was sent before the SETTINGS frame.)

Continuing with the output:

```
[  0.164] send HEADERS frame <length=45, flags=0x05, stream_id=1>
         ; END_STREAM | END_HEADERS ❹
         (padlen=0)
         ; Open new stream
         :method: GET
         :path: /
         :scheme: https
         :authority: www.akamai.com
         accept: */*
         accept-encoding: gzip, deflate
         user-agent: nghttp2/1.9.2
         header1: Foo ❺
```

This shows the header block for the request.

❹ Note the client (nghttp) sent the END_HEADERS and END_STREAM flags. This tells the server that there are no more headers coming and to expect no data.

---

6 *https://github.com/nghttp2/nghttp2*

Had this been a POST, for example, the END_STREAM flag would not have been sent at this time.

❺ This is the header we added on the `nghttp` command line.

```
[  0.171] recv SETTINGS frame <length=30, flags=0x00, stream_id=0> ❻
         (niv=5)
         [SETTINGS_HEADER_TABLE_SIZE(0x01):4096]
         [SETTINGS_MAX_CONCURRENT_STREAMS(0x03):100]
         [SETTINGS_INITIAL_WINDOW_SIZE(0x04):65535]
         [SETTINGS_MAX_FRAME_SIZE(0x05):16384]
         [SETTINGS_MAX_HEADER_LIST_SIZE(0x06):16384]
[  0.171] send SETTINGS frame <length=0, flags=0x01, stream_id=0> ❼
         ; ACK
         (niv=0)
[  0.197] recv SETTINGS frame <length=0, flags=0x01, stream_id=0>
         ; ACK
         (niv=0)
```

❻ Ngtttpd received the server's SETTINGS frame.

❼ Sent and received acknowledgment of the SETTINGS frames.

```
[  0.278] recv (stream_id=1, sensitive) :status: 200 ❽ ❾
[  0.279] recv (stream_id=1, sensitive) last-modified: Wed, 01 Jun 2016 ...
[  0.279] recv (stream_id=1, sensitive) content-type: text/html;charset=UTF-8
[  0.279] recv (stream_id=1, sensitive) etag: "0265cc232654508d14d13deb...gzip"
[  0.279] recv (stream_id=1, sensitive) x-frame-options: SAMEORIGIN
[  0.279] recv (stream_id=1, sensitive) vary: Accept-Encoding, User-Agent
[  0.279] recv (stream_id=1, sensitive) x-akamai-transformed: 9 - 0 pmb=mRUM,1
[  0.279] recv (stream_id=1, sensitive) content-encoding: gzip
[  0.279] recv (stream_id=1, sensitive) expires: Wed, 01 Jun 2016 22:01:01 GMT
[  0.279] recv (stream_id=1, sensitive) date: Wed, 01 Jun 2016 22:01:01 GMT
[  0.279] recv (stream_id=1, sensitive) set-cookie: ak_bmsc=70A833EB...
[  0.279] recv HEADERS frame <length=458, flags=0x04, stream_id=1> ❿
         ; END_HEADERS
         (padlen=0)
         ; First response header
```

Here we have the response headers from the server.

❽ The `stream_id` of 1 indicates which request it is associated with (we have only sent one request, but life is not always that simple).

❾ Nghttpd got a 200 status code from the server. Success!

❿ Note that this time the END_STREAM was not sent because there is DATA to come.

```
[  0.346] recv DATA frame <length=2771, flags=0x00, stream_id=1> ⓫
[  0.346] recv DATA frame <length=4072, flags=0x00, stream_id=1>
```

```
[ 0.346] recv DATA frame <length=4072, flags=0x00, stream_id=1>
[ 0.348] recv DATA frame <length=4072, flags=0x00, stream_id=1>
[ 0.348] recv DATA frame <length=1396, flags=0x00, stream_id=1>
[ 0.348] send WINDOW_UPDATE frame <length=4, flags=0x00, stream_id=1>
```

⑪   At last we got the data for the stream. You see five DATA frames come down followed by a WINDOW_UPDATE frame. The client indicated to the server that it consumed 10,915 bytes of the DATA frames and is ready for more data. Note that this stream is not done yet. But the client has work to do and thanks to multiplexing it can get to it.

```
[ 0.348] send HEADERS frame <length=39, flags=0x25, stream_id=15> ⑫
          :path: /styles/screen.1462424759000.css
[ 0.348] send HEADERS frame <length=31, flags=0x25, stream_id=17>
          :path: /styles/fonts--full.css
[ 0.348] send HEADERS frame <length=45, flags=0x25, stream_id=19>
          :path: /images/favicons/favicon.ico?v=XBBK2PxW74
```

⑫   Now that the client has some of the base HTML, it can start asking for objects on the page. Here you see three new streams created, IDs 15, 17, and 19 for stylesheet files and a favicon. (Frames were skipped and abbreviated for clarity.)

```
[ 0.378] recv DATA frame <length=2676, flags=0x00, stream_id=1>
[ 0.378] recv DATA frame <length=4072, flags=0x00, stream_id=1>
[ 0.378] recv DATA frame <length=1445, flags=0x00, stream_id=1>
[ 0.378] send WINDOW_UPDATE frame <length=4, flags=0x00, stream_id=13>
          (window_size_increment=12216)
[ 0.379] recv HEADERS frame <length=164, flags=0x04, stream_id=17> ⑬
[ 0.379] recv DATA frame <length=175, flags=0x00, stream_id=17>
[ 0.379] recv DATA frame <length=0, flags=0x01, stream_id=17>
          ; END_STREAM
[ 0.380] recv DATA frame <length=2627, flags=0x00, stream_id=1>
[ 0.380] recv DATA frame <length=95, flags=0x00, stream_id=1>
[ 0.385] recv HEADERS frame <length=170, flags=0x04, stream_id=19> ⑬
[ 0.387] recv DATA frame <length=1615, flags=0x00, stream_id=19>
[ 0.387] recv DATA frame <length=0, flags=0x01, stream_id=19>
          ; END_STREAM
[ 0.389] recv HEADERS frame <length=166, flags=0x04, stream_id=15> ⑬
[ 0.390] recv DATA frame <length=2954, flags=0x00, stream_id=15>
[ 0.390] recv DATA frame <length=1213, flags=0x00, stream_id=15>
[ 0.390] send WINDOW_UPDATE frame <length=4, flags=0x00, stream_id=0>
          (window_size_increment=36114)
[ 0.390] send WINDOW_UPDATE frame <length=4, flags=0x00, stream_id=15> ⑭
          (window_size_increment=11098)
[ 0.410] recv DATA frame <length=3977, flags=0x00, stream_id=1>
[ 0.410] recv DATA frame <length=4072, flags=0x00, stream_id=1>
[ 0.410] recv DATA frame <length=1589, flags=0x00, stream_id=1>    ⑮
[ 0.410] recv DATA frame <length=0, flags=0x01, stream_id=1>
[ 0.410] recv DATA frame <length=0, flags=0x01, stream_id=15>
```

Here we see the overlapping streams coming down.

⓭ You can see the HEADERS frames for streams 15, 17, and 19.

⓮ You see the various window updates, including a connection-level update for stream 0.

⓯ The last DATA frame for stream 1.

```
[  0.457] send GOAWAY frame <length=8, flags=0x00, stream_id=0>
          (last_stream_id=0, error_code=NO_ERROR(0x00), opaque_data(0)=[])
```

Finally we get the GOAWAY frame. Ironically this is the polite way to tear down the connection.

The flow may seem cryptic at first, but walk through it a few times. Everything logically follows the spec and has a specific purpose. In this straightforward example you can see many of the elements that make up h2, including flow control, multiplexing, and connection settings. Try the nghttp tool yourself against a few h2-enabled sites and see if you can follow those flows as well. Once it starts to make sense you will be well on your way to understanding the protocol.

Summary

The HTTP/2 protocol was many years in development and is full of design ideas, decisions, innovations, and compromises. This chapter has provided the basics for being able to look at a Wireshark dump (see "Wireshark" on page 115) of h2 and understand what is going on, and even find potential problems in your site's use of the protocol (constantly changing cookie, perhaps?). For those who would like to go deeper, the ultimate resource is the RFC 7540 itself.[7] It will provide every detail needed for the implementor, debugger, or masochist that lurks inside you.

---

7 *https://tools.ietf.org/html/rfc7540*

CHAPTER 6

HTTP/2 Performance

One of the goals of HTTP/2 was improved performance. For some, this is the only reason to switch over. Though h2 will generally be faster than HTTP/1.1 for web page delivery, it is not always the case. Understanding the conditions that affect h2's performance is an important part of tuning your site and understanding end users' experiences. Many variables need to be taken into consideration when measuring the performance of h2, and this assesment goes well beyond classifications of "slower" or "faster." This chapter will explore the most important factors that contribute to real-world HTTP/2 performance.

Client Implementations

HTTP/2 is a young protocol and as is often the case, implementations, though spec compliant, can vary in subtle but important ways. For example, browsers like Chrome, Firefox, Safari, and Microsoft Edge all have different quirks that may affect a user's experience on your site. The performance of the same website using different clients from within the same network connection can show considerable differences in page load times. Understanding these differences can be a critical part of tuning your site for the largest possible audience.

Akamai's Foundry Team performed a study of HTTP/1.1 versus HTTP/2 performance with a goal of understanding how different browsers compare. It involved looking at billions of Real User Monitoring (RUM) measurements from real devices under real network conditions. The results showed differences between the browsers, and for the most part h2 requests were faster than h1 requests (Figure 6-1).

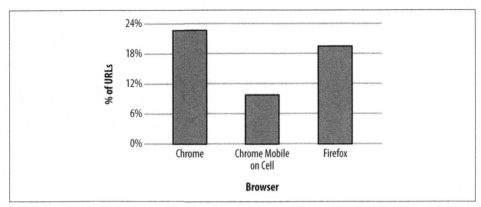

Figure 6-1. Percentage of URLs with a statistically significant performance improvement with HTTP/2

Mission accomplished, right? As it turns out, no. The study also showed that some URLs experienced a drop in performance when running h2 (see Figure 6-2 for details).

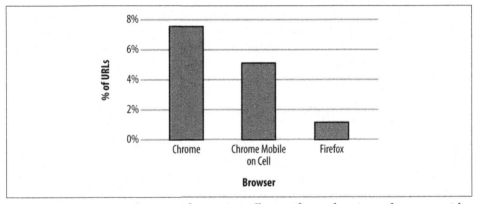

Figure 6-2. Percentage of URLs with a statistically significant drop in performance with HTTP/2

Why would h2 ever be slower? It is important to understand that the study was look-ing at individual requests, not full page loads. That means the only room for improvement lies in header compression, connection reuse, and an avoidance of head of line blocking. Items such as multiplexing and Server Push, which are more focused on improving the performance of a group of requests on a page, will not have an effect. Even so, many more URLs show a performance improvement with h2 versus a loss. The difference in the data highlights two important points: first, implementa-tions matter, and second, not all requests will benefit from HTTP/2 under all circum-stances.

Latency

In computer networks, latency is how much time it takes for a packet of data to get from one point to another. It is sometimes expressed as the time required for a packet to travel to the receiver and back to the sender, or Round-Trip Time (RTT), and it is generally measured in milliseconds (ms).

Many factors contribute to latency, but two of the more influential are the distance between the two points and the speed of the transmission medium used. For wired networks those mediums are generally made of optical fiber and/or copper wires, while mobile/wireless networks leverage radio waves. To determine the theoretical smallest latency between two points, you need to look at the speed of light in those mediums and the length of the lines between them. For example, the speed of light in optical fiber is about 2/3 the speed of light in a vacuum or around 200,000,000 meters per second. So if you stretched a fiber-optic cable straight from San Francisco to London, which is around 8500 km, you would have a lowest possible latency of about 43 ms. The only way to lower that latency would be to bring the endpoints closer together (or develop a faster medium).

Regardless of advances in transmission mediums, the speed of light is a hard limit. Thus, bringing the two endpoints closer together has the most opportunity for improving latency. Continental drift may take care of the SF → London problem in time, but the impatient who prefer to not work in geological timescales may want to deploy servers closer to their end users around the world or leverage a CDN (see "Content Delivery Networks (CDNs)" on page 95).

Of course, if you check you will never actually see a latency measurement that low. First, the networks are not laid out in straight lines. Second, delays are introduced by the various gateways, routers, switches, cell towers, etc. (as well as your server application itself), that your data needs to pass through in order to get from A to B.

More Bandwidth Doesn't Matter (Much)

Mike Belshe (the coinventor of the SPDY protocol) published a study in 2010 titled "More Bandwidth Doesn't Matter (Much)"[1] about the effect of bandwidth and RTT on the loading time of web pages.

His testing showed that an increase in bandwidth correlated with an improvement on web page download time; however, the performance improvement decreases once the bandwidth reaches 5 Mbps, and almost flattens completely at around 8 Mbps or

---

1 *http://bit.ly/2pO5Nu2*

more. On the other hand, page load time (PLT) goes down exponentially as the RTT decreases (in the study, each 20 ms decrease on RTT yielded a 7% to 15% reduction in PLT).

In a nutshell: decreasing RTT, regardless of current bandwidth, always helps make web browsing faster.

The graphs in Figure 6-3 (taken from the study) illustrate the effects of both bandwidth and RTT on page load times.

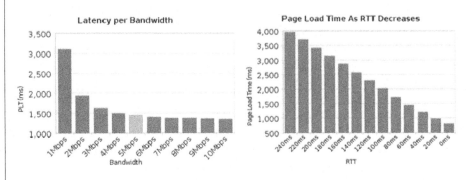

Figure 6-3. Effects of bandwidth and RTT on PLT

You can measure the latency between a client and a server easily by using the `ping` command tool, which is available in most operating systems.

Here's how to use the `ping` command to measure the RTT to the Wikipedia website:

```
$ ping -c 4 www.wikipedia.org
PING www.wikipedia.org (208.80.154.224) 56(84) bytes of data.
64 bytes from text-lb.eqiad.wikimedia.org (...): icmp_req=1 ttl=50 time=70.4 ms
64 bytes from text-lb.eqiad.wikimedia.org (...): icmp_req=2 ttl=50 time=70.7 ms
64 bytes from text-lb.eqiad.wikimedia.org (...): icmp_req=3 ttl=50 time=70.5 ms
64 bytes from text-lb.eqiad.wikimedia.org (...): icmp_req=4 ttl=50 time=70.5 ms

--- www.wikipedia.org ping statistics ---
4 packets transmitted, 4 received, 0% packet loss, time 3002ms
rtt min/avg/max/mdev = 70.492/70.571/70.741/0.284 ms
```

The `ping` command was run from a client computer located in San Jose, California. According to GEO location data, the server IP 208.80.154.224 that was hosting Wikipedia was located in Ashburn, VA (about 3850 km or 2392 miles apart from the client in California).

Table 6-1 provides sample average latency values, depending on the transport medium.

Table 6-1. Latency values by transport media

Media type	Average RTT
Fiber	17–22 ms
Cable	15–30 ms
DSL	32–52 ms
Mobile Networks	40-1000 ms depending on the wireless technology like LTE (fastest), HSPA, or GSM/Edge (slowest)
Satellite	600–650 ms

 Be aware that some mobile devices may turn off the mobile radio for short periods of time to save battery, which can add up to several seconds of latency for new connections if the device has to wake up the mobile radio hardware.

To measure the impact of latencies in h2, we configured a simple website that represents an average web page of the top 1000 websites in terms of size, in bytes, and number of objects. We then used a CDN (see "Content Delivery Networks (CDNs)" on page 95) in front of the site so that we could manually hit servers in different areas of the world to get a variety of "real" latencies. Using the free web-based performance testing tool Web Page Test (aka WPT; see "WebPagetest" on page 109) we loaded the page over h1 and h2 using Chrome and Firefox agents.

Table 6-2 shows the impact of latency on page load time when using h1 versus h2. The PLT times are the average of repeating the test 20 times over a period of 2 days; each test consists of 9 "First View" WPT runs.

Table 6-2. h1 versus h2 performance by real latency using WPT's agent: Dulles - Cable

Origin location	Latency	h1 PLT Chrome (ms)	h2 PLT Chrome (ms)	h1 PLT Firefox (ms)	h2 PLT Firefox (ms)
New York, USA	15 ms	4518	5064	4673	4637
Montreal, Canada	39 ms	4719	5325	4815	4718
Dallas, TX, USA	42 ms	4728	4986	4965	4995
Paris, France	97 ms	6248	5765	5634	5402
Cairo, Egypt	129 ms	6873	5272	5266	5256
Rio de Janeiro, Brasil	142 ms	7302	5932	6055	6220

One thing that should jump out from the data is that generally, as the distance from the origin increases and hence the latency, the performance of h2 relative to h1 improves.

Packet Loss

Packet loss happens when packets of data traveling across a computer network fail to reach their destination; this is usually caused by network congestion. Packet loss is measured as a percentage of packets lost with respect to the number of packets sent. High packet loss has a detrimental impact on pages delivered over h2, mostly because h2 opens a single TCP connection, and the TCP protocol reduces the TCP window size each time there is loss/congestion (see "Inefficient use of TCP" on page 17).

A recent study on HTTP/2 performance in cellular networks[2] by the University of Montana and Akamai's Foundry team analyzed the effect of packet loss on different types of content (small objects and larger objects).

The study found that:

- For web pages containing many small objects (365 x 2 KB), page load times over h2 are faster than over h1, because in the case of h1 (with six TCP connections) the server can only send six objects in parallel (due to head of line blocking), whereas in h2 many streams can be multiplexed over one connection. Further, as the network condition becomes poor, the PLTs increase for both h1 and h2—but the effect is more dramatic for h2. This is due to the single connection architecture. When that one connection is hit by loss, the whole works slows down (see the lefthand graph in Figure 6-4).

- For web pages containing a small number of larger objects (10 x 435 KB), h1 outperforms h2 across all network conditions. This possibly surprising finding is because of the initial congestion window (see Figure 3-4). With six connections opened, h1 effectively has six times the initial congestion window size as h2. That means it can get much more data faster early on in the session as the h2 connection window grows to its optimal size. There is ongoing work to address this limitation as it results in initial congestion windows being too small for h2, yet arguably too large for h1. And again, loss has a bigger effect on h2 than h1 (see the righthand graph in Figure 6-4).

- For web pages with a couple of extremely large objects, the differences disappear. The h2 initial congestion window disadvantage is mitigated by the length of the overall download, and its multiplexing does not really have an advantage any longer.

The majority of web pages fall into the first bucket (they contain many small objects) where h2 has the biggest advantage. This is no accident as it is precisely the use case the designers were optimizing for. Regardless, packet loss is h2's Achilles heel.

---

2 *http://akamai.me/2oEPSOZ*

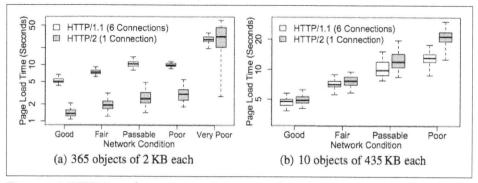

(a) 365 objects of 2 KB each (b) 10 objects of 435 KB each

Figure 6-4. HTTP/2 performance in cellular networks

Where Is My HTTP/2 Performance?

Web Page Test is an incredible tool (see "WebPagetest" on page 109), but the one thing it lacks is the ability to easily get a statistically significant amount of data. Running a few tests on your site can give you a rough feel for things and show you where some problems might be, but it is hard to answer the general question of "Is my site faster?" when you are looking at 10% to 20% gains over a small data set. Tools like Catchpoint, Keynote, and Gomez can get you a higher volume of tests to look at and are definitely as great step up from one-off tests, but they are still what is called *synthetic testing* as opposed to real traffic.

What you really want to know is what performance your users are seeing. Your real users. Hence Real User Monitoring (RUM) is the standard for performance statistics gathering. You can look at doing it yourself with tools like Boomerang, or you can reach out to companies like SOASTA or Speedcurve. However you go about getting RUM results, that data is a gold mine waiting to be, well, mined.

Once you have your data, look at it in terms of percentiles and not averages. None of your users are average, but some of them have better or worse experiences. Looking at the median performance will tell you that 50% of users have better (or worse) performance than that. Jumping up to the 95th or even 99th percentile shows you some of the worst experiences your users are having. Thinking about performance this way allows you to target certain segments and monitor how your changes affect them.

And h2? We usually see an improvement at the median and a much larger improvement at the 95th and upper percentiles. That 95th percentile improvement may mean the difference between a user staying and using your site or abandoning it and going to a competitor. Focusing on the worst performing aspects of your site's performance can have a great business impact. This all means that h2's tag line could just as well be, "It will make your site suck less." But then that isn't terribly catchy.

Server Push

As discussed in "Server Push" on page 53, Server Push gives the server the ability to send an object to a client before the client requests it. Testing has shown push speeding up page render times by as much as 20% to 50% if used properly.

However, push can also waste bandwidth as the server may try to push objects that the client already has in the local cache, causing the client to receive extra bytes that it does not need. The client can send RST_STREAM frames in order to reject the server's PUSH_PROMISE frames, but due to the timing of the frames the server generally will end up sending out the unwanted data regardless.

The true value of Server Push is achieved when pushing the critical CSS and JS objects needed for rendering a page the first time someone visits it. The server implementation needs to be smart enough to avoid push promises competing for bandwidth with the delivery of the base HTML page, however. Ideally, the server will push while it is processing the request for the base HTML page. At times, the server needs to do some backend work to generate the HTML. While it is thinking and the client is waiting, there is a perfect opportunity to start pushing down objects that the client will need. See Figure 6-5 for an illustration of how this can improve performance.

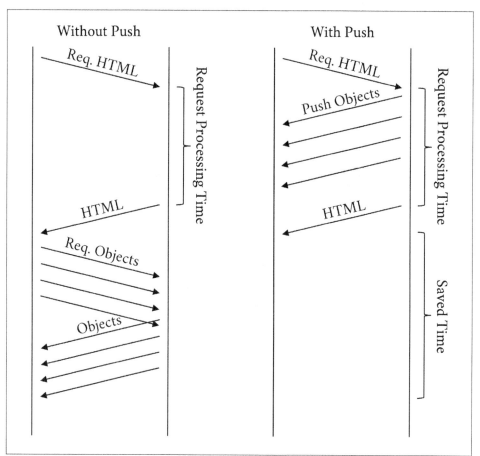

Figure 6-5. Push while processing

Does My Client and Server Support Server Push?

Colin Bendell shared during a talk at the Velocity Amsterdam conference in 2016 a simple but effective website called *canipush.com* that allows you to see if your client supports Server Push.

Table 6-3 shows some the output of that page for the most popular browsers.

Table 6-3. Push support by browsers

Browser	Chrome 54.0	Firefox 50.0.1	Safari iOS 10.1	Edge
HTTP/2 enabled	PASS	PASS	PASS	PASS
Current host PUSH JavaScript	PASS	PASS	PASS	PASS
Current host PUSH CSS	PASS	PASS	PASS	PASS
Current host PUSH XHR	PASS	PASS	PASS	FAIL
Connection coalescing JavaScript	PASS	PASS	FAIL	FAIL
Connection coalescing CSS	PASS	PASS	FAIL	FAIL
Connection coalescing XHR	FAIL	FAIL	FAIL	FAIL

Time to First Byte (TTFB)

Time to First Byte (TTFB) is a measurement used as an indication of the responsiveness of a web server.

TTFB measures the duration from the client making an HTTP request to the first byte of the object being received by the client's browser. This duration is a combination of the socket connection time, the time taken to send the HTTP request, and the time taken to get the first byte of the page. Although sometimes misunderstood as a post-DNS calculation, the original calculation of TTFB in networking always includes network latency in measuring the time it takes for a resource to begin loading.

In h1 the client requests one object at a time per hostname per connection, and the server sends those objects in order, one after the other. Once the client receives all the objects, it requests the next set of objects, and the server sends them, and this process continues until the client receives all the objects needed to render the page.

However, with h2 multiplexing, once the client has loaded the HTML, it will send a much higher number of simultaneous requests to the server as compared to h1. In aggregate these requests will generally return in a shorter amount of time than with h1, but since the clock starts sooner for the requested objects, the TTFB for those will be reported as higher. So, because the mechanics of how the protocols work are different, the meaning of TTFB changes from h1 to h2.

HTTP/2 does do a bit more work than h1, the goal of which is to gain better overall performance. Here are a few of the things h2 does that h1 doesn't:

- Adjusting window sizes
- Building the dependency tree
- Maintaining static and dynamic tables of header information
- Compressing and decompressing headers
- Adjusting priorities (h2 allows a client to adjust the priority several times for a single request)
- Pushing additional streams not requested yet by the client

Figures 6-6 and 6-7 show a clear picture of the advantage of h2 over h1. To produce the results shown in those figures, the same page was loaded over h1 and h2. Though some of the metrics such as TTFB and "Time to Title" may be comparable or in h1's favor, the overall experience is better with h2.

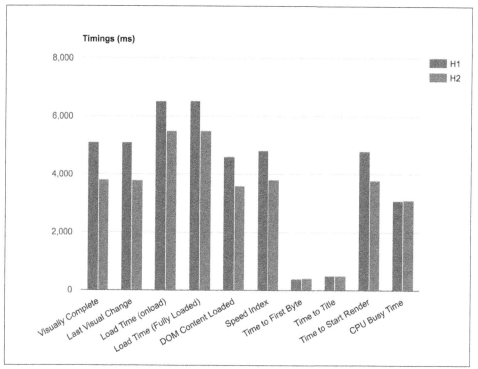

Figure 6-6. Timings h1 versus h2

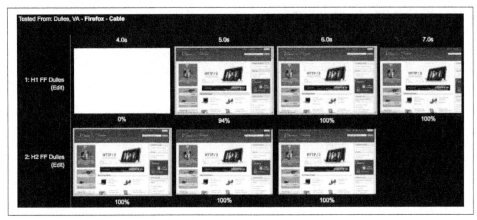

Figure 6-7. Page rendering h1 versus h2

Third Parties

Many websites today use analytics, tracking, social, and advertising platforms that must be added to the website using snippets of code called third-party tags. Third-party tags are snippets of code provided by third-party vendors, and which generate browser calls to external third-party servers.

Numerous studies show that third-party calls can slow down your site, and even cause it to fail like in the case of blocking JavaScript. Pages that have a significant amount of third-party content showed no significant improvement in performance over h2. Third-party content can affect performance in general, but it affects h2 especially because:

- A third-party request is delivered over a different hostname, which causes a performance hit as the browser needs to resolve DNS, establish a TCP connection, and negotiate TLS.

- Due to being on a different hostname, the request won't be able to benefit from h2 features like Server Push, dependencies, and priorities as it is reserved for objects on the same hostname only.

- You can't control the performance of the third party or whether the resource is delivered over h2.

Another way to think of it is if third-party content accounts for half of your page's load time, then h2 can only address half of any performance problems.

In the context of a web page, a Single Point Of Failure, or SPOF, is a resource of a web page that, if it fails, will delay (and even cause to fail) the loading of the entire web page. Pat Meenan, a software engineer and performance expert known for his work on the Web-PageTest platform, created a very useful Google Chrome browser extension called SPOF-O-MATIC,[3] which easily allows detecting SPOFs as you surf pages and visualize the impact they can cause using WebPagetest. It is yet another great tool to add to your debugging arsenal.

To test the impact of third-party calls on performance, we set up four simple HTML pages, each of them with just five images loading from a given hostname. The HTML body looks like this:

```
<html>
  <head lang="en">
    <meta http-equiv="Content-Type" content="text/html; charset=UTF-8">
    <title>What is your Ikigai?</title>
  </head>
  <body>
    <img src="https://akah1san.h2book.com/what.png">
    <img src="https://akah1san.h2book.com/is.png">
    <img src="https://akah1san.h2book.com/your.png">
    <img src="https://akah1san.h2book.com/ikigai.png">
    <img src="https://akah1san.h2book.com/question-mark.png">
  </body>
</html>
```

The hostname of the images is changed to control whether h1 or h2 is used. Test cases were created by varying the following parameters:

- Whether the base page is on h2 or h1
- Whether the objects are on h2 or h1
- Whether the hostnames for the objects are on the same certificate as the base page (hence allowing connection coalescing)

Although the results are pretty similar due to the small number of objects, we can see the images starting to show up 100 ms earlier when using h2 due to only having to open a single connection, as seen in Figure 6-8. The savings will increase as the latency to the server increases.

---

3 *https://github.com/pmeenan/spof-o-matic*

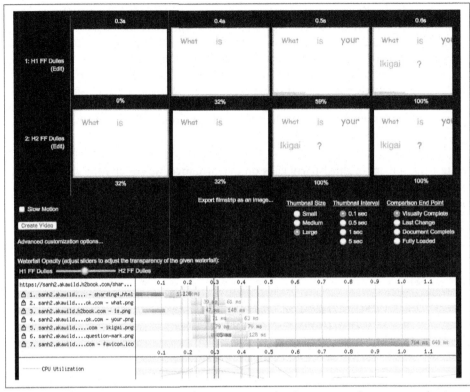

Figure 6-8. WPT filmstrip and timeline comparing loading a page that uses two host-name shards on h1 versus h2

We can see the impact on performance of opening more connections in h1 more clearly if we increase the number of domain shards to four with the same number of objects per domain. The HTML was modified from the previous example to repeat the same five images over three additional hostnames (note that all four hostnames are part of the same SAN certificate):

```html
<html>
  <head lang="en">
    <meta http-equiv="Content-Type" content="text/html; charset=UTF-8">
    <title>What is your Ikigai?</title>
  </head>
  <body>
    <img src="https://akah2san.h2book.com/what.png">
    <img src="https://akah2san.h2book.com/is.png">
    <img src="https://akah2san.h2book.com/your.png">
    <img src="https://akah2san.h2book.com/ikigai.png">
    <img src="https://akah2san.h2book.com/question-mark.png">
    <img src="https://akah2san1.h2book.com/what.png">
    <img src="https://akah2san1.h2book.com/is.png">
```

```
<img src="https://akah2san1.h2book.com/your.png">
<img src="https://akah2san1.h2book.com/ikigai.png">
<img src="https://akah2san1.h2book.com/question-mark.png">
<img src="https://akah2san2.h2book.com/what.png">
<img src="https://akah2san2.h2book.com/is.png">
<img src="https://akah2san2.h2book.com/your.png">
<img src="https://akah2san2.h2book.com/ikigai.png">
<img src="https://akah2san2.h2book.com/question-mark.png">
<img src="https://akah2san3.h2book.com/what.png">
<img src="https://akah2san3.h2book.com/is.png">
<img src="https://akah2san3.h2book.com/your.png">
<img src="https://akah2san3.h2book.com/ikigai.png">
<img src="https://akah2san3.h2book.com/question-mark.png">
</body>
</html>
```

Figure 6-9 shows the results of loading the preceding web page. You can see that the page delivered over h2 loads roughly 25% faster.

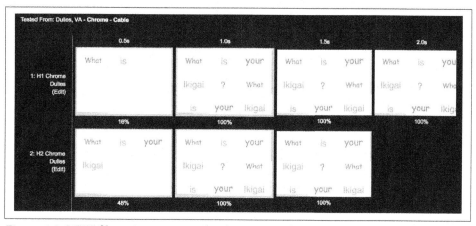

Figure 6-9. WPT filmstrip comparing loading a page that uses four hostname shards on h1 versus h2

If we take a deeper look at the timeline for the page loaded over h1 (Figure 6-10), you will see most of connections loading the embedded images start with indicators of the initial connection and SSL handshake time. This shows the cost of opening multiple connections under h1.

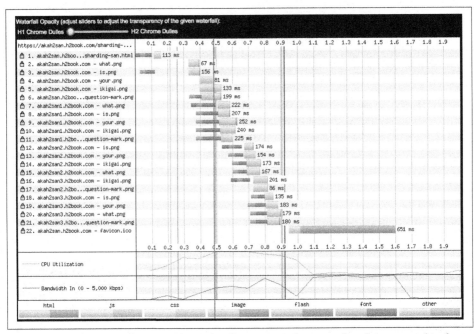

Figure 6-10. WPT timeline comparing loading a page that uses four hostname shards using h1

On the other hand, when the page loads over h2 (Figure 6-11) only the first object is preceded by time spent doing connection and TLS establishment, meaning the rest of objects were sent over the same connection.

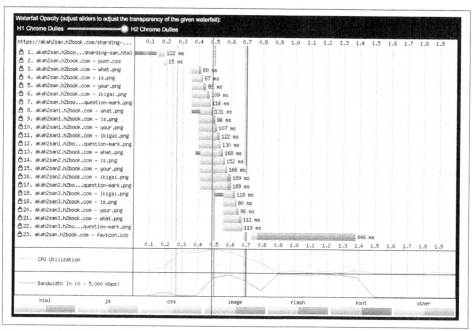

Figure 6-11. WPT timeline comparing loading a page that uses four hostname shards using h2

The exercises described in this section show that it is possible to migrate a website that uses domain sharding to h2 and achieve a single connection by means of grouping different hostnames under a common certificate, and benefiting from the *connection coalescence* implemented by browsers like Chrome and Firefox.

HTTP/2 Anti-Patterns

As seen in "Undoing HTTP 1.1 'Optimizations,'" some of the h1 performance patterns become anti-patterns in h2. This section reviews the more common of those workarounds and describes the performance implications of using them in h2.

Domain Sharding

Sharding aims at leveraging the browser's ability to open multiple connections per hostname to parallelize asset download and overcome the sequential nature of h1. It is quite common to see sharding on sites with many small objects leveraging the six connections or so that modern web browsers open per hostname. This "tricks" the browser into sending more requests in parallel and makes more use of the available bandwidth. Because of HTTP/2's use of multiplexing, sharding is unnecessary and defeats the goals the protocol is trying to achieve. Connection coalescing (see "Connection Coalescing" on page 92) has the potential to remove the sharding in some browsers under certain conditions, but it is best to not rely on this and instead avoid sharding in h2 altogether.

Inlining

Inlining involves inserting JavaScript, stylesheets, and even images into an HTML page with the aim of saving extra connections and round-trips required to load external resources. Some of the best practices for web performance, however, recommend against inlining, as you lose valuable features like caching that usually help reduce the number of requests (and speed up page render) on repeat visits of the same page. However, in general there can sometimes still be value in inlining small resources needed to render the above-the-fold region. In fact, there is evidence that on weaker devices, the overhead of requests might outweigh the benefits of caching.

The general rule is avoid inlining with h2, but it may not always be without benefit. (See "Your Mileage May Vary" on page 83 for more info.)

Concatenating

Concatenating means consolidating several small files into a single larger file. It is very similar to inlining as it aims to save round-trips when loading external resources, and device CPU when decoding or evaluating scripts over a fewer number of objects. The same concepts we see for inlining apply for concatenating. Use it to consolidate very small files (1 KB or less), and for the minimum amount of JavaScript/CSS that is critical for the initial rendering.

Cookie-less Domains

Serving static content from a cookie-less domain is a standard performance best practice, especially since in h1 you can't compress headers, and some websites use cookies that often exceed the size of a TCP packet. In h2, however, request headers are compressed using the HPACK algorithm, which considerably reduces the size of large cookies (especially when they don't change across requests). Furthermore, cookie-less domains require using additional hostnames, which means opening more connections.

If you are using cookie-less domains, you may consider undoing it next time you have a chance. If you don't really need them, then best to leave them off. Every byte saved matters.

Spriting

Spriting is yet another technique for avoiding many requests for small objects (you can see a trend in what people do to optimize h1). To sprite, a developer lays out a matrix of smaller images in a larger image and then uses CSS to choose which portion of the image to show. Depending on the device and its hardware graphics capability, spriting can be very efficient or quite slow. With h2, the best practice is to avoid spriting as multiplexing and header compression take a lot of the request overhead away, but there may still be circumstances where you can find spriting beneficial.

Your Mileage May Vary

If at this point you are frustrated with this section and its conditional council couched in carefully constructed caveats, it is understandable. To maximize your web performance you need to balance a host of variables, including network conditions, device capabilities, browser abilities, *and* protocol limitations. These combine into what we call *situations*, and there are more situations to consider than most developers have time for.

So what to do? The best practice to rule them all: *test*. Performance testing and monitoring is critical to getting the most out of anything, and HTTP/2 is no exception. Look at your real user data, slice and dice across various conditions, look for problems, and then address them. Follow industry recommendations, but do not fall victim to pre-optimization. Let your data direct your fine-tuning efforts.

Prefetch

Prefetching is a web performance optimization that "hints" the browser to go ahead and download a cacheable object "whenever possible," and store it on the browser's cache. However, the browser can ignore prefetch requests if busy, or if the asset takes too long to download. Prefetch consists of inserting a *link* tag in the HTML:

```
<link rel="prefetch" href="/important.css">
```

or a Link header in the HTTP response:

```
Link: </important.css>; rel=prefetch
```

Prefetch is less relevant with h2 with the introduction of Server Push, which can get an object down to the browser faster. One advantage of prefetch over push is that if the object is already in cache, the browser will not waste time and bandwidth requesting it. Think of it as a tool that can complement h2 push as opposed to something that is replaced by it.

Real-World Performance

Theory and tests are great up to a point, but the IETF has a saying that "*code speaks and data speaks louder.*" Let's look at a couple of real-world websites using HTTP/2 and see how they perform.

Performance Measurement Methodology

Our performance testing methodology consisted of using WPT (see "WebPagetest" on page 109) and running each website through several of the following:

Test Locations
Geographically dispersed test locations (US West Coast, US East Coast, and Europe)

Browsers
Chrome and Firefox (chosen because they allow you to easily disable h2, allowing A/B testing)

Connections
Simulated network connections (Cable and Fast 3G)

Test runs
Each test was run nine times (in order to get a good average)

This means we ran 108 WPT tests (3 x 2 x 2 x 9) against each of the websites. This methodology is far from perfect and conclusive, and it is meant to provide guidance for folks interested in running their own basic performance tests without making a big investment of time and resources.

 This section makes heavy use of WebPagetest results and requires access to those results to get the most out of it. To play along at home, follow the links in the text and enjoy.

Study 1: www.facebook.com

The engineers at Facebook manage to get consistent improvements on the tests with h2 versus h1. It is evident that they spent some time tuning their delivery for h2. For example, they configured their servers to undo domain sharding on their home page when the client requests it over h2 to maximize the benefits of multiplexing on a single connection that using h2's prioritization provides.

In terms of perceived performance, the main Facebook page over h2 started displaying 33% faster, a whopping 1.5 seconds earlier than over h1 (see Figure 6-12). Open *http://goo.gl/m8GPYO* to see this test.

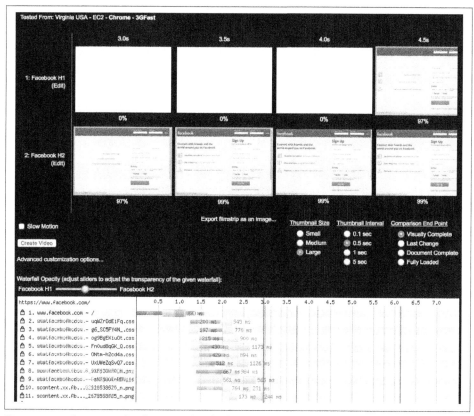

Figure 6-12. h1 versus h2 for www.facebook.com on simulated 3G conditions

If you take a deeper look at the waterfalls in Figure 6-12, you will see the main reason for this difference is the single TCP connection of h2—on the h1 waterfall you can see the performance penalty of opening six extra connections. See the waterfall for h2 (*http://goo.gl/w4vSLg*) when compared to h1 (*http://goo.gl/sWjL3M*).

If you inspect the waterfall for the h2 test, you will see that most of the critical objects for rendering are loaded from the same hostname as the one delivering the HTML (www.facebook.com). In the h1 version, the HTML loads from www.facebook.com, but most of the stylesheets and JavaScript load from static.xx.fbcdn.net. Although in this case the performance penalty was caused by h1 opening extra TCP connections, if you click the h2 waterfall on the embedded objects, you will see WPT displaying dependencies and priorities like those listed in Table 6-4. (Note the WPT agent was Chrome. This is important, as at the time of writing, WPT displays stream information differently depending on the selected browser.)

Table 6-4. HTTP/2 dependencies and priorities (weights)

URL	Priority	HTTP/2 stream information (dependencies)
https://www.facebook.com/	VeryHigh	1, weight 256, depends on 0, EXCLUSIVE
https://www.facebook.com/rsrc.php/v3/yE/r/uqWZrDdEiFq.css	High	3, weight 220, depends on 0, EXCLUSIVE
https://www.facebook.com/rsrc.php/v3/yQ/r/g6_SC5FY4N_.css	High	5, weight 220, depends on 3, EXCLUSIVE
https://www.facebook.com/rsrc.php/v3/yD/r/og9BgEKiuOt.css	High	7, weight 220, depends on 5, EXCLUSIVE
https://www.facebook.com/rsrc.php/v3/yn/r/FnOud8qGK_Q.css	High	9, weight 220, depends on 7, EXCLUSIVE
https://www.facebook.com/rsrc.php/v3/yE/r/ONtm-h2cd4a.css	High	11, weight 220, depends on 9, EXCLUSIVE
https://www.facebook.com/rsrc.php/v3/yG/r/UxUWeZqSvQ7.css	High	13, weight 220, depends on 11, EXCLUSIVE
https://www.facebook.com/rsrc.php/v3/yh/r/sXFjOOknRDN.js	Medium	15, weight 183, depends on 13, EXCLUSIVE
https://www.facebook.com/rsrc.php/v3/yb/r/GsNJNwul-UM.gif	VeryLow	17, weight 110, depends on 15, EXCLUSIVE
https://scontent.xx.fbcdn.net/t39.2365-6/851565_602269956474188_918638970_n.png	VeryLow	1, weight 110, depends on 0, EXCLUSIVE
https://scontent.xx.fbcdn.net/t39.2365-6/851585_216271631855613_2121533625_n.png	VeryLow	3, weight 110, depends on 0, EXCLUSIVE
https://scontent.xx.fbcdn.net/t39.2365-6/851558_160351450817973_1678868765_n.png	VeryLow	5, weight 110, depends on 3, EXCLUSIVE
https://www.facebook.com/rsrc.php/v2/ye/r/Oqx-vnsuxPL.png	VeryLow	19, weight 110, depends on 0, EXCLUSIVE

...

Study 2: www.yahoo.com

HTTP/2 looks great on www.yahoo.com. The h2 page for yahoo.com starts being displayed in 4 seconds, while the h1 version starts displaying in 5.5 seconds (see Figure 6-13). Open *http://goo.gl/eRUilp* to see this test.

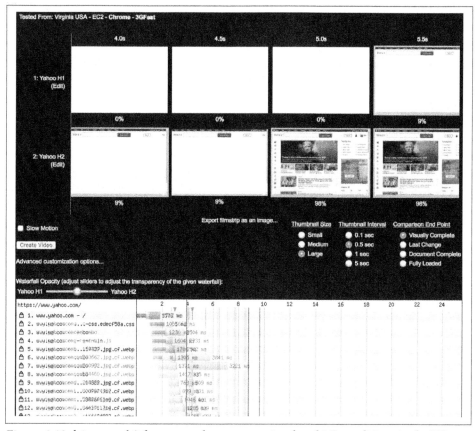

Figure 6-13. h1 versus h2 for www.yahoo.com on simulated 3G conditions in the US

Similar to the Facebook example, www.yahoo.com loads resources differently depending on whether the client negotiates h2 or h1. HTTP/2 delivers the HTML and assets both on www.yahoo.com, while when using h1, the HTML is delivered using www.yahoo.com and the assets using s.yimg.com. With h1 the browser opens six connections for the s.yimg.com hostname, which causes a considerable delay. Also the page elements load in a different order over h2, causing faster DOM complete and PLT, as seen in Figure 6-13. The Yahoo website showed positive improvements when loaded from WPT agents in the US. Interestingly, h1 loads much faster when using a WPT agent in Ireland. The h2 page starts being displayed in 7.5 seconds, while the h1 version starts displaying in 4.5 seconds. See *https://goo.gl/GrySYa* for details.

You can see in Figure 6-14 that it seems Yahoo's home page in Ireland is generated slightly differently than its US counterpart. In this case the domain sharding has not been undone when loading the page over h2. Most of the embedded objects (like, for example, *http://bit.ly/2pOgTiG*) are delivered over a different domain than the one delivering the base HTML. The data shows that a couple of the runs took significantly longer with h2, which skewed the averages.

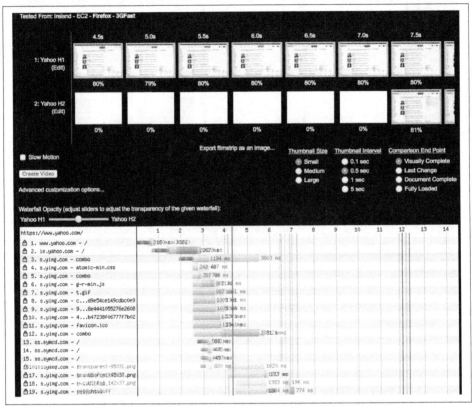

Figure 6-14. h1 versus h2 for www.yahoo.com on simulated 3G conditions in Ireland

But why was h2 slower? It could be dismissed with the wave of a hand and some statistical mumbo jumbo about small data sets and lack of significance, but that would be hiding an extremely important point: h2 will not always be faster in every case. The use of multiple connections (rather than one) and network conditions are the likely culprit in this particular case; a dropped packet could have thrown everything off. Other times the cause will be the makeup of the site. Or, in these early days of h2, it could also be undiscovered implementation bugs. Regardless, seeing performance drop in certain cases is to be expected, and it is almost always addressable.

Summary

It is highly probable that you picked up this book because performance matters to you. HTTP/2 delivers that performance, but it is important to understand why that is, and why you might not be seeing it. Just like any other performance effort, there are likely to be cycles of code, test, analyze, and optimize. Even if you turn on h2 and your site is performing better than ever, a bit of sleuthing might reveal even more performance waiting to be unleashed.

CHAPTER 7

HTTP/2 Implementations

A contributor to the success of HTTP/2 is the support it received in terms of the number of implementations available in mainstream tools. Even before the RFC was finalized, a significant portion of the internet user base was talking h2 behind the scenes, unknowingly reaping the benefits of the "next best thing to hit the web." Support was not limited to a fringe of experimental browsers and web servers. Rather, the most popular browsers, servers, proxies, caches, and command-line tools included h2 early on. Understanding what is available and what options exist for the various implementations is important for your development plan, whether its goal is targeting your web user base, or choosing a web server or proxy.

As the internet moves faster than the speed of the written word, there is no chance we will hit every functionality corner case or list every supporting piece of software. This chapter will at least serve as an overview of features to look for and a good place to start in your selection efforts.

Desktop Web Browsers

Browsers are developed so that you do not *need* to understand anything about h2 in order to use it. Everyone who uses a modern popular web browser is already using h2 on a daily basis. HTTP/2 causes things to work slightly differently than before, however, and understanding those differences and the different features that surround them can be important for your development and debugging efforts.

TLS Only

All browsers mentioned in this chapter require the use of TLS (HTTPS) in order to speak HTTP/2. This is despite the fact that the HTTP/2 specification itself does not require TLS. See "Is TLS Required?" on page 36 for a discussion on this topic.

Disabling HTTP/2

HTTP/2 is new, and because of that, when encountering problems you may want to try testing your site with it turned off. Or perhaps you want to look at your request waterfalls with h2 on and with h2 off. In either case you need a way to turn HTTP/2 on and off in a browser. Unfortunately, not all browsers give you this ability. Table 7-1 indicates which ones do.

Table 7-1. Browser support

Browser	First HTTP/2 Version	Disable	Push	Coalescing	Debugging	Beta channel
Chrome	41 (Mar 2015)	Yes	Yes	Yes	Yes	Yes
Firefox	36 (Feb 2015)	Yes	Yes	Yes	Yes	Yes
Microsoft Edge	12 (July 2015)	No	Yes	No	Yes	Yes
Safari	9 (Sep 2015)	No	Yes	No	No	Yes
Opera	28 (Mar 2015)	Yes	Yes	Yes	Yes	Yes

Support for HTTP/2 Server Push

Server Push is one of the most exciting features in h2, and one of the hardest to use correctly. Since it is not needed for simple delivery of pages it is sometimes left out in initial h2 implementations. All the major browsers (see Table 7-1) support this feature.

Connection Coalescing

Support for connection coalescing can improve the performance of requests by causing existing connections to be reused when previously a new one would have been needed to be established. This means the TCP and TLS handshakes can be skipped, improving the performance of the first request to the new host. Browsers that support coalescing will first check to see if they have a connection that happens to go to the same place before opening a new one. In this case, *same place* means that the certificate on the existing connection is valid for the new hostname and the hostname resolved to the IP address of that connection. Under those conditions, the browser will send HTTP/2 requests for the new host on the already established connection.

HTTP/2 Debugging Tools

When working with h2 it is at times important to be able to see what is going on behind the scenes. Some browsers have great support specifically for h2 in their toolset. See Chapter 8 for a deep dive on that topic.

Beta Channel

Though not strictly an HTTP/2 feature, having access to beta (or earlier) versions of a browser can be a great way to stay ahead of changes and play with the bleeding edge of protocol development.

See canisue.com[1] for a comprehensive, up-to-date list of browsers that support h2.

Mobile

Mobile browsers generally closely follow on the heels of their desktop brethren these days (Table 7-2).

Table 7-2. Mobile browser support

Browser	Operating system	First HTTP/2 version	Push	Coalescing
Chrome	iOS	41 (Mar 2015)	Yes	No
Safari	iOS	9.2 (Sep 2015)	Yes	No
Chrome	Android	12 (July 2015)	Yes	Yes
Android	Android	53 (Oct 2016)	Yes	Yes
Microsoft Edge	Windows Mobile	12 (July 2015)	Yes	No

No mobile browser at this point supports turning h2 support off.

Mobile App Support

Following the XCode update in June 2015,[2] Apple included h2 support in iOS using NSURLSession by default, with app transport security allowing native iOS apps to benefit from the h2 protocol. For Android apps to benefit from h2, the app needs to use an h2-capable library like OkHttp[3] and connect to an h2-capable web server over TLS.

---

1 *http://caniuse.com/#search=http2*

2 *https://lukasa.co.uk/2015/06/HTTP2_Picks_Up_Steam_iOS9/*

3 *http://square.github.io/okhttp/*

Servers, Proxies, and Caches

When it comes to serving content over h2 you have a number of choices. HTTP/2-enabled endpoints come in two basic flavors:

Web server
> Traditional processes that serve static and dynamic content.

Proxy/cache
> A process that sits between a server and an end user. It can be used to offload a web server (via caching), add additional processing, or both. Many proxies can also fill the role of a web server.

These are often used together to create high-performing websites with high availability; though for smaller sites a proxy layer may be unnecessary.

There are a number of critical areas to examine and evaluate when choosing a server for HTTP/2. Beyond the basics of general performance, OS support, personal knowledge, scalability, and stability, you should also look at support for *Server Push* and *dependencies/priorities*.

Push is generally implemented in one of two ways: static inclusion of files and triggering off of *link* headers and tags. Neither of these methods is perfect, but if configured carefully they can have a positive impact on performance. Perfect push requires coordination with the browser to know what is in its cache to avoid unnecessary pushes. No server supports that—at least not yet.

Using Link

One method for a server to communicate to a proxy what to push is to send a *Link* header for each element that should be pushed. Details vary between server and proxy types, but in general adding the following to a response:

```
Link: </script.js>; rel=preload
```

will communicate that *script.js* should be pushed.

Proper support of dependencies and priorities is one of the most important tools for getting the most out of HTTP/2 for web performance. This is where much of the "science" goes into building an h2-capable server. It may be worthwhile testing a few servers against a few different browsers to get a feel for what is performing best for your use case.

Table 7-3 summarizes the common servers and their capabilities as of this writing.

Table 7-3. HTTP/2-capable endpoints

Server	Type	Push
Apache	Server	Yes
Nginx	Server / Proxy / Cache	No
IIS	Server	Yes
Jetty	Server	Yes
h2o	Server / Proxy	Yes
Squid	Proxy / Cache	Yes
Caddy	Sever	No
Varnish	Proxy / Cache	No
Traffic Server	Proxy / Cache	Yes

Content Delivery Networks (CDNs)

A Content Delivery Network (CDN) is a globally distributed network of reverse proxy servers deployed in multiple data centers. The goal of a CDN is to serve content to end users with high availability and high performance mostly by being closer to the average end user and therefore reducing the round-trip network latency. CDNs are a critical cog in the performance and scaling of the internet. They range from "free to use" for low-volume web properties up through enterprise class services that provide performance, reliability, and security to some of the largest web properties on the planet.

Most major CDNs support HTTP/2, though overall protocol support and functionality vary somewhat between them. Similar to looking at web servers, two of the most important areas to examine are support for push and how they handle priorities. Those items can make a world of difference when it comes to real-world performance.

Summary

It is remarkable how much support exists today for h2 considering how young the protocol is. The most popular web servers, proxies, and CDNs—as well as over 70% of all browsers in use—already fully support h2. On the other hand, h2 features like Server Push are still on earlier stages, and tuning around dependencies and priorities continues to evolve. We will undoubtedly see advances on these fronts in the near future.

CHAPTER 8

Debugging h2

Spending nearly 2 decades with a protocol means 20 years of tools for monitoring and debugging. Now HTTP/2 comes along, and your old way of doing things no longer works. This could be a mission-critical blocker until tools are updated or replaced. Regardless, h2 is a different though vaguely similar beast to h1. Much of what worked before will work now, but the differences are important. Fortunately, there is already a rich supply of test and debugging tools available, ranging from things that are specific to HTTP/2 to updates to your current toolsets that you already use.

Web Browser Developer Tools

Most modern web browsers include web developer tools that are useful for debugging h2. The following sections are a few examples of how you can follow an h2 stream, identify h2 priorities and dependencies, and understand Server Push using Chrome and Firefox Developer Tools. Note that similar concepts can be applied to other popular browsers like Safari, Edge, or Opera.

Chrome Developer Tools

Over the past few years the Chrome browser has gained adoption among web developers in part due to the increasing functionality of its Web Developer tools.[1] Being familiar with their capabilities can provide you an advantage for solving your next technical snafu. Pull up the developer tool by choosing View → Developer → Developer Tools in the Chrome menu.

---

1 *http://bit.ly/2oRIK40*

Net internals

Chrome net-internals[2] can be accessed by typing `chrome://net-internals` in Chrome's address bar. These tools provide a look at the network data, including capturing/exporting/importing low-level network data, checking network and DNS logs, and visualizing network activity.

The net-internal tools can be used to capture HTTP/2 traffic, which is useful to illustrate some HTTP/2 concepts like:

- Stream IDs
- Priorities
- Dependencies
- Server-Push promises
- Session PINGs

Here are the steps to do a capture of HTTP/2 traffic:

1. Type **`chrome://net-internals`** in Chrome's address bar.
2. Select HTTP/2 from the left sidebar.
3. Open a new tab and type the your favorite URL in the address bar.
4. Go back to the net-internals tab, where you will see a list of all the active sessions to hostnames that use the HTTP/2 protocol.
5. Click the ID link located on the right side of the hostname of the entered URL (see Figure 8-1).

---

2 *http://bit.ly/2pvAzvI*

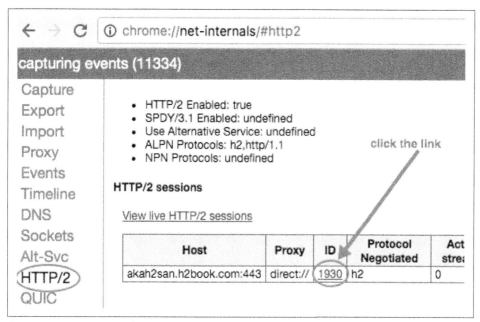

Figure 8-1. Net-internals HTTP/2

6. The context will change to Events. Click the checkbox located on the left side of the hostname (Figure 8-2).

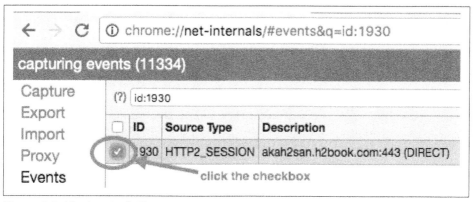

Figure 8-2. Net-internals Events

7. On the right side of this page you should see a capture of all the traffic between the web server and the client.

Let's review some of the fields used in the capture. Each "event" starts with something like this:

```
t=timestamp [st=  milliseconds]    EVENT_TYPE
```

For example:

```
t=123808 [st=   1]    HTTP2_SESSION_SEND_HEADERS
```

- The first field "t" indicates the timestamp, in milliseconds, since the browser session started. For example, a value of 123808 indicates the HTTP/2 session has started 123.8 seconds after the browser's session started.

- The second field "st" indicates the relative number of milliseconds since the HTTP/2 session started. For example, a value of 1 indicates the event happened 1 millisecond after the HTTP/2 was started.

- The third field shows the type of event recorded.

Some of the Chrome h2 events correspond directly to h2 frame types. For example, HTTP2_SESSION_RECV_PUSH_PROMISE indicates a PUSH_PROMISE frame type, an HTTP2_SESSION_PING corresponds to a PING frame, and so on.

Let's look at a sample capture to give you a feel for how to read them and to see what HTTP/2 information we can pull out:

```
t=791301 [st=   1]    HTTP2_SESSION_SEND_HEADERS ❶
                      --> exclusive = true
                      --> fin = true              ❷
                      --> has_priority = true     ❸
                      --> :method: GET            ❹
                          :authority: akah2san.h2book.com
                          :scheme: https
                          :path: /
                          cache-control: max-age=0
                          upgrade-insecure-requests: 1
                          user-agent: Mozilla/5.0 (Macintosh; Intel Mac...
                          accept: text/html,application/xhtml+xml,...
                          accept-encoding: gzip, deflate, sdch, br
                          accept-language: en-US,en;q=0.8
                          cookie: [30 bytes were stripped]
                          if-none-match: "11168351bd3324ad3e43ed68195063c5:1464989325"
                      --> parent_stream_id = 0    ❺
                      --> stream_id = 1           ❻
                      --> weight = 256            ❼

    ...
```

❶ Here is the event information line as described previously

❷ fin = true indicates that there is no additional head frame coming

❸ This request has priorities set

❹ The HTTP headers on the frame start here

❺ The associated parent stream in stream 0

❻ This stream has ID 1 (the first client request)

❼ The relative weight for dependencies is 256

By looking at the net-internal events you can get a clear picture of precisely what is happening when and even look inside the protocol.

 If reading this output from Chrome makes you cross-eyed, you are not alone—and there is help. Rebecca Murphy created a brilliant little tool called *chrome-http2-log-parser* (*http://bit.ly/2oIjhd5*) that, as she says, takes the HTTP/2 net-internals output and turns "it into something more useful." We agree.

Server Push visualization

The Network tab of Chrome's Developer Tools panel is useful for visually following the communication between the client and the server, while displaying a bunch of useful information in a table format like:

- Object's name
- Object's size
- Status code
- Priority
- Total load time
- Breakdown of load times within a timeline

Let's look at an example. Load the web page *https://akah2san.h2book.com/* (a simple page that loads over HTTP/2 and uses Server Push).

In the Network tab, you should see something like Figure 8-3.

Figure 8-3. Server Push timeline

The Network tab tells us that the HTML loads three stylesheets and four PNG images. From those seven objects, two of them (*/resources/push.css* and */resources/ http2-banner-0614.png*) are "pushed" to the client, while the other five load normally.

If we mouse over one of the objects in the waterfall on the righthand side of the pane, we will see a breakdown on the different stages while the object was fully loaded. Here is the explanation of the information displayed (see Figure 8-4):

- Connection Setup
    - Queueing: Time the request was postponed by the rendering engine or network layer.
    - Stalled: Time the request spent waiting before it could be sent.
- Request/Response
    - Request Sent: Time spent issuing the network request.
    - Waiting (TTFB): Time spent waiting for the initial response, also known as the Time To First Byte. This number captures the latency of a round-trip to the server in addition to the time spent waiting for the server to deliver the response.
    - Content Download: Time spent receiving the response data.
- Total time (labeled *Explanation*)

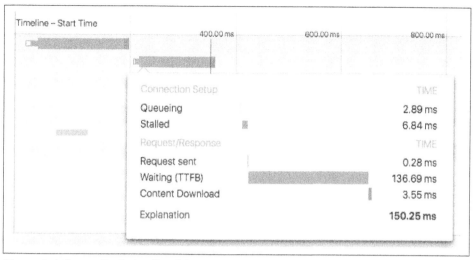

Timeline – Start Time		
Connection Setup		TIME
Queueing		2.89 ms
Stalled		6.84 ms
Request/Response		TIME
Request sent		0.28 ms
Waiting (TTFB)		136.69 ms
Content Download		3.55 ms
Explanation		150.25 ms

Figure 8-4. Server Push timeline h2.css

If we mouse over one of the objects that are pushed by the server, we will see the information shown in Figure 8-5:

- Server Push
  - — Receiving Push: Time it takes to receive all the bytes for the pushed object
- Connection Setup
  - — Queueing: Time the request was postponed by the rendering engine or network layer
- Request/Response
  - — Reading Push: Time it takes for the browser to read the bytes pushed from the temporary cache
- Total time (labeled *Explanation*)

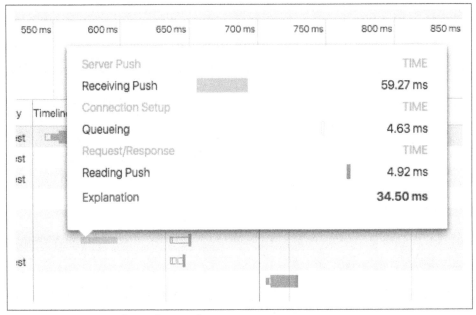

Figure 8-5. Server Push timeline push.css

Chrome session key logging

Both Chrome and Firefox provide the ability to log the TLS session key used for encrypting particular encrypted connections in the browser. It is incredibly useful for using external tools such as Wireshark (see "Wireshark" on page 115) to examine the traffic and look at the HTTP/2 frames. This functionality is triggered by setting the appropriate environment variable to the location you want the keys logged before you launch the browser. For example, on OS X you could do:

```
$ SSLKEYLOGFILE=~/keylog.txt
$ open /Applications/Google\ Chrome.app/Contents/MacOS/Google\ Chrome
```

Mozilla has a good description of this process written up at *https://devel oper.mozilla.org/en-US/docs/Mozilla/Projects/NSS/Key_Log_Format*.

Firefox Developer Tools

The Firefox browser provides a variety of tools to help web developers. In the next few sections we'll describe some of Firefox's features that are useful to debug web content delivered over HTTP/2.

Logging HTTP sessions

Logging HTTP sessions can be useful for debugging purposes, and Firefox's HTTP Session logging can provide you a lot of insight into what is going on over the wire.

There is no *in-browser* mechanism for getting those captures from Firefox at this time. A bit of command-line hacking is required.

Let's use Firefox's HTTP Session logging to do a capture of HTTP/2 traffic, which will illustrate some HTTP/2 concepts like:

- Stream IDs
- Priorities
- Dependencies
- Server-Push promises
- Session PINGs

To enable logging, use the following commands in the Windows command prompt:

```
cd c:\
set NSPR_LOG_MODULES=timestamp,nsHttp:5,nsSocketTransport:5,nsStreamPump:5, ^
    nsHostResolver:5
set NSPR_LOG_FILE=%TEMP%\firefox_http_log.txt
cd "Program Files (x86)\Mozilla Firefox"
.\firefox.exe

or MAC OS terminal:

export NSPR_LOG_MODULES=timestamp,nsHttp:5,nsSocketTransport:5, \
    nsStreamPump:5,nsHostResolver:5
export NSPR_LOG_FILE=~/Desktop/firefox_http_log.txt
cd /Applications/Firefox.app/Contents/MacOS
./firefox-bin
```

 A text file called *firefox_http_log.txt* will be saved in the directory indicated by the shell variable NSPR_LOG_FILE. If you set the variable GECKO_SEPARATE_NSPR_LOGS=1, each child process will get logged to its own file. Each log file will have the name you specify in the NSPR_LOG_FILE environment variable, but with the string ".child-X" appended to it, where X is a different number for each child process.

You can control the verbosity of the log file by updating the values of the shell variable NSPR_LOG_FILE in a couple of ways:

- Reducing the number on the right of the module. For example, nsHttp:3 indicates less verbosity than nsHttp:5. See Table 8-1 for a list of debug values.
- Removing a module from the list. For example, NSPR_LOG_MODULES=time stamp,nsHttp:5 is less verbose than NSPR_LOG_MODULES=timestamp,nsHttp:

5,nsSocketTransport:5,nsStreamPump:5. You can get the most verbose logging by using NSPR_LOG_MODULES=all:5.

See Firefox Log Modules (*https://mzl.la/2pcgU2o*) for a more comprehensive list of modules that can be included in the logs.

Table 8-1. NSPR_LOG_FILE verbosity levels

Level	Description
0	nothing should be logged
1	important; intended to always be logged
2	errors
3	warnings
4	debug messages, notices
5	everything!

Firefox session key logging

Firefox, like Chrome, can log the TLS session keys. See "Chrome session key logging" on page 104 for a description.

Debugging h2 on iOS Using Charles Proxy

Debugging h2 on iOS is not straightforward due to TLS encryption, the iOS security model, and a general lack of visibility. This section explains how to debug iOS devices by using a computer running Charles Proxy.[3] Charles Proxy is, as its name implies, a proxy. By configuring your devices to go through this proxy you can see precisely what requests and responses are occurring. This is what you already get in browsers like Chrome and Firefox, but is lacking for browsers like Safari on iOS, and native iOS applications.

You need to use Charles Proxy version 4 (or higher) to ensure HTTP/2 support. Additionally, though an excellent tool worthy of adding to your toolbox, Charles Proxy is not free. For the purposes of trying it out and following along with the book, a time-limited trial version is available. A free alternative would be to use nghttp2 (see "nghttp2" on page 110) in proxy mode.

---

3 *https://www.charlesproxy.com/*

The debugging process consists on installing Charles Proxy on a machine, then installing its root certificate on the device you want to proxy (so Charles Proxy can "man in the middle" and decrypt TLS traffic), and finally configuring the proxy settings on the iOS device to point to the IP and port of the host computer running Charles Proxy. We'll explain how to do this using an iOS Simulator, and using an actual iOS device.

iOS Simulators

To get Charles Proxy set up to debug h2 in an iOS Simulator running on the same machine, follow these steps:

1. Quit your iOS Simulator.
2. Launch Charles Proxy.
3. Open the Help menu and choose SSL Proxying → Install Charles Root Certificate in iOS Simulators (this will install it into all of your local iOS Simulators).

Now when you start the iOS Simulator, you should be able to access TLS websites with Charles Proxy using TLS Proxying.

iOS devices

In order to debug HTTPS traffic on iOS devices you need to run a proxy on a computer and change the iOS device network settings to use the proxy running on that computer.

 It is best to use a dedicated iOS device for debugging as installing the Charle's Proxy root certificate may replace any existing configuration profiles on the iOS device.

On the host computer:

1. Start Charles Proxy.
2. On the Proxy menu select Proxy Settings and ensure the port is set to 8888 (you can use Dynamic Port if you have problems connecting to the 8888 port).
3. On the Proxy menu select SSL Proxy Settings, click Add, and type the hostname you want to monitor on the Host field (or use * to monitor any site).
4. On the Proxy menu select Access Control Settings and add the IP of the iOS device (or just 0.0.0.0/0 to allow all devices to connect).

5. On the Help menu select Local IP Address, write down your local IP address, and close the window (you will need to use that IP as a proxy server on the iOS device).

6. On the File menu select New Session to start recording traffic.

For more information on this process, see *https://www.charlesproxy.com/documenta tion/proxying/ssl-proxying/*.

Next, on the iOS device:

1. Open the Settings app → "Wifi settings," and then click the Information icon that looks like (i) located on the right of the WiFi network you are connected to.

2. In the list that appears, scroll down to the HTTP PROXY section and select Manual.

3. In the Server field that appears, put the IP of the host computer, and in the port field put 8888 (or enter a different number if you are using a dynamic port).

4. Click the home button, start Safari, and point the browser to chls.pro/ssl (or *http://www.charlesproxy.com/getssl/*) to install Charles's proxy root certificate (needed to decrypt TSL traffic).

Now you should be able to access TLS websites with Charles using SSL Proxying (except for apps that use pinned certificates–like some Apple native apps).

Debugging h2 on Android

You have to do a small amount of setup before you can start debugging h2 on Android. On the Android device open up Settings, find the Developer options section, and enable USB debugging (if you're running Android 4.2 or later and you can't find Developer options, you may need to enable it[4]).

Once you have done that, on your development computer:

1. Open Chrome (and make sure you are logged in to one of your user profiles, as this debugging method does not work in incognito or guest mode).

2. Choose View → Developer → Developer Tools and select More tools → Remote devices from the "…" menu on the right. From here you can see the status of all connected remote devices (make sure that Discover USB devices is enabled).

3. Connect your Android device using a USB cable to a USB port on your development computer (don't use any USB hubs).

---

4 *http://bit.ly/2pvN5uw*

4. Authorize the connection on the Android device the first time you connect it to the computer by tapping the "Allow USB debugging" prompt on your Android device and grant the permissions. Once you authorize the device you will see the Android Device as Connected.

You can now inspect traffic on the device. You can also enable the "toggle screencast" button to view the screen of your Android device from within your DevTools panel.

WebPagetest

WebPagetest is a free web-based performance monitoring tool for measuring various aspects of a website's performance. It leverages server farms of web browsers distributed around the world, allowing you to test how your site performs under various different network conditions and browser types. Other features that are worth noting are:

- Ability to script a test in various ways to emulate a full browser session
- Saving filmstrips and videos of the web page loading for later comparison across runs
- Getting full packet traces for use in tools like Wireshark (see "Wireshark" on page 115)
- Adjusting various network parameters to limit bandwidth, increase latency, and introduce loss

It is a great way to see how your changes might perform in a wide variety of situations. It is a subject that requires much more detail than can be provided here, and for that detail we recommend checking out the book *Using WebPagetest*, by Rick Viscomi, Andy Davies, and Marcel Duran (O'Reilly) to learn more.

OpenSSL

OpenSSL[5] is an open source implementation of the SSL and TLS protocols in the form of a software library (delivered over Apache and BSD license agreements) that allows applications to secure communications. This section focuses on the command-line tool also known as openssl, and how to use it to debug HTTP/2.

---

5 *https://www.openssl.org/*

OpenSSL Commands

Since many web browsers only support HTTP/2 over HTTPs, the openssl command is useful for verifying whether a web server's SSL certificate meets all the requirements for HTTP/2. Here's how you check (just replace "akah2san.h2book.com" with the hostname you want to check):

```
$ echo | openssl s_client -connect \
        akah2san.h2book.com:443 -servername akah2san.h2book.com \
        -alpn spdy/2,h2,h2-14 | grep ALPN
...
ALPN protocol: h2
```

 The | grep ALPN command at the end filters the output to just a couple of lines. If you omit that, you will see the full output from the openssl s_client command, which has information that is useful for debugging your TLS configuration. It includes your certificate chain, your certificate, what ciphers are negotiated, ALPN negotiation, and a variety of other details. Spend some time with this tool and it will pay you back handsomely.

nghttp2

nghttp2 (*https://nghttp2.org/*) is an implementation of HTTP/2 and its header compression algorithm HPACK in C.

The framing layer of HTTP/2 is implemented as a form of reusable C library. On top of that, nghttp2 provides the tools listed in Table 8-2.

Table 8-2. nghttp2 tools

Tool	Description
nghttp	A command-line client
nghttpd	A server
nghttpx	A proxy
h2load	A load testing tool
inflatehd	HPACK command-line header decompression tool
deflatehd	HPACK command-line header compression tool

This section focuses on the command-line client, known as nghttp.

Using nghttp

You can use nghttp to debug an HTTP/2 URL and display HTTP/2 frame information.

Some useful parameters you can pass to nghttp are:

- -v (prints debug information)
- -n (discards downloaded data like HTML bodies)
- -a (downloads embedded assets indicated on the HTML that are delivered over the same hostname)
- -s (prints statistics)
- -H <header> (adds a header to the request, for example: -H':method: PUT')
- --version (displays version information, and exits)

> Use nghttp --help to see a list of all the available parameters.

The following command shows an example of using nghttp with the n and s parameters to discard the downloaded data, and download statistics, respectively:

```
$ nghttp -ns https://akah2san.h2book.com/hello-world.html
***** Statistics *****

Request timing:
  responseEnd: the time when last byte of response was received
               relative to connectEnd
 requestStart: the time just before first byte of request was sent
               relative to connectEnd.  If '*' is shown, this was
               pushed by server.
      process: responseEnd - requestStart
         code: HTTP status code
         size: number of bytes received as response body without
               inflation.
          URI: request URI

see http://www.w3.org/TR/resource-timing/#processing-model

sorted by 'complete'

id  responseEnd requestStart  process code size request path
 2   +142.85ms *    +35.89ms 106.96ms  200   64 /resources/push.css
13    +175.46ms       +128us 175.33ms  200  169 /hello-world.html
```

If you examine the preceding output, you may notice a couple of interesting items as a result of HTTP/2 Push:

- Here, */resources/push.css* was downloaded although the parameter a was not indicated. That was because that asset was pushed by the server as the * on the requestStart indicates.

- */resources/push.css* was downloaded *before* the HTML itself.

A complete example of using nghttp and examining the output can be found in "A Simple GET" on page 58.

curl

curl[6] is a software project originally authored by Daniel Stenberg providing a library (libcurl) and command-line tool (curl) for transferring data using various protocols. Though it uses the nghttp2 libraries for its HTTP/2 support, it is much more common than nghttp and different enough to merit its own slot in your debugging toolbox. As of the time of writing, curl was available in 261 packages, across 34 operating systems. You can use the curl download wizard[7] to help find the right package for you.

Using curl

To use curl with HTTP/2, pass in the --http2 option on the command line. Adding -v will provide some rich debugging data on whatever URL you specify. Much of the information we were able to get using the openssl tool is made readily available in the verbose curl output. Here is an example:

```
$ curl -v --http2 https://akah2san.h2book.com/hello-world.html
*   Trying 2001:418:142b:19c::2a16...
* Connected to akah2san.h2book.com (2001:418:142b:19c::2a16) port 443 (#0)
* ALPN, offering h2                                    ❶
...
* SSL connection using TLSv1.2 / ECDHE-RSA-AES256-GCM-SHA384
* ALPN, server accepted to use h2
* Server certificate:                                  ❷
*   subject: CN=akah2san.h2book.com
*   start date: Aug 12 17:59:00 2016 GMT
*   expire date: Nov 10 17:59:00 2016 GMT
*   subjectAltName: host "akah2san.h2book.com" matched cert's
      "akah2san.h2book.com"
*   issuer: C=US; O=Let's Encrypt; CN=Let's Encrypt Authority X3
*   SSL certificate verify ok.
* Using HTTP2, server supports multi-use
* Connection state changed (HTTP/2 confirmed)
```

---

6 *https://github.com/curl/curl/*

7 *https://curl.haxx.se/dlwiz/*

```
...
* Using Stream ID: 1 (easy handle 0x7f8d59003e00)  ❸
> GET /hello-world.html HTTP/1.1
> Host: akah2san.h2book.com
> User-Agent: curl/7.49.1
> Accept: */*
>
* Connection state changed (MAX_CONCURRENT_STREAMS updated)!
* HTTP 1.0, assume close after body
< HTTP/2 200                                        ❹
< server: Apache
< content-length: 169
...
<
<html>                                              ❺
        <head lang="en">
                <meta http-equiv="Content-Type" content=
                "text/html; charset=UTF-8">
                <title>Hello HTTP/2</title>
        </head>
        <body>Hello HTTP/2</body>
</html>
* Closing connection 0
* TLSv1.2 (OUT), TLS alert, Client hello (1):
```

❶ ALPN information

❷ TLS information (similar to what we saw with openssl)

❸ Stream data

❹ We used HTTP/2 and we got a 200 response. Life is good.

❺ The page content

Measuring page load times

You can use curl's w parameter to print useful performance metrics (see the curl man page[8] for reference).

By adding the following parameter to a curl request (note that the parameter includes some text formatting):

```
-w "Connection time: %{time_connect}\t1st byte transfer:
  %{time_starttransfer}\tDownload time: %{time_total}
    (sec)\tDownload Speed: %{speed_download} (bps)\n"
```

---

8 *https://curl.haxx.se/docs/manpage.html*

you will see metrics like:

- Connection time
- First byte time
- Download time
- Total time
- Download speed (indicating how many bytes you can send per second)

For example:

```
$ curl -v --http2 https://akah2san.h2book.com/hello-world.html -w \
    "Connection time: %{time_connect}\t                              \
    1st byte transfer: %{time_starttransfer}\t                       \
    Download time: %{time_total} (sec)\t                             \
    Download Speed: %{speed_download} (bps)\n"

...omitting a bunch of lines...
* Connection #0 to host akah2san.h2book.com left intact
Connection time: 0.054  1st byte transfer: 0.166  Download time: 0.166 (sec)
Download Speed: 1016.000 (bps)
```

h2i

h2i[9] is an interactive HTTP/2 console debugger created by Brad Fitzpatrick, which allows sending "raw" HTTP/2 frames to the server. It will allow you to interact with an HTTP/2 server directly in much the same way you could do with h1 previously with tools like telnet or openssl.

h2i just requires indicating the hostname of a website that supports HTTP/2. Once you connect you will see an h2i> prompt, which allows sending HTTP/2 frames to the server.

The following example shows using the h2i client to request *https://www.google.com/* (note that long lines are truncated with <cut> as needed):

```
$ h2i www.google.com
Connecting to www.google.com:443 ...
Connected to 172.217.5.100:443
Negotiated protocol "h2"
[FrameHeader SETTINGS len=18]
  [MAX_CONCURRENT_STREAMS = 100]
  [INITIAL_WINDOW_SIZE = 1048576]
  [MAX_HEADER_LIST_SIZE = 16384]
[FrameHeader WINDOW_UPDATE len=4]
```

---

9 *https://github.com/bradfitz/http2/tree/master/h2i*

```
     Window-Increment = 983041

h2i> headers
(as HTTP/1.1)> GET / HTTP/1.1
(as HTTP/1.1)> Host: www.google.com
(as HTTP/1.1)>
Opening Stream-ID 1:
 :authority = www.google.com
 :method = GET
 :path = /
 :scheme = https
[FrameHeader HEADERS flags=END_HEADERS stream=1 len=445]
  :status = "200"
  date = "Wed, 01 Mar 2017 00:08:06 GMT"
  expires = "-1"
  cache-control = "private, max-age=0"
  content-type = "text/html; charset=ISO-8859-1"
  p3p = "CP=\"This is not a P3P policy! See <cut>
  server = "gws"
  x-xss-protection = "1; mode=block"
  x-frame-options = "SAMEORIGIN"
  set-cookie = "NID=98=OOy2zBP3TY9GM37WXG9PFtN <cut>
  alt-svc = "quic=\":443\"; ma=2592000; v=\"35,34\""
  accept-ranges = "none"
  vary = "Accept-Encoding"
[FrameHeader DATA stream=1 len=16384]
  "<!doctype html><html itemscope=\"\" itemtype=\"http://schema.org/WebPage\"
   lang=\"en\"> <head><meta content=\"Search the world's information, including
   webpages, images, videos and more. Google has many special features to help
   <cut>
[FrameHeader PING len=8]
  Data = "\x00\x00\x00\x00\x00\x00\x00\x00"
h2i> quit
```

Wireshark

Wireshark[10] is a popular network packet analyzer with a built-in understanding of hundreds of higher-level protocols, including HTTP/2. This means it can not only pull packets off the wire similar to venerable tools like tcpdump, it can reassemble those packets into the higher-level protocol you want to examine. It comes in the form of a GUI as well as a command-line tool called tshark.

The Wireshark website[11] has binaries for Windows and macOS for download and simple installation. In addition there are links to port and packages for another 20 or so various Unix/Linux flavors. It is well supported and easy to get.

---

10 *https://www.wireshark.org/*

11 *https://www.wireshark.org/download.html*

Using Wireshark to look at h2 is made complicated by the fact that most all HTTP/2 is over TLS. This means in a Wireshark dump you will see TLS packets but the sniffer will not be able to see inside those packets. This is the general idea behind TLS, after all. In "Firefox session key logging" on page 106 and "Chrome session key logging" on page 104 we discussed how to get Firefox and Chrome to log the keying material so Wireshark can use it to look inside the TLS packet. That feature plus the HTTP/2 plug-in that currently ships with Wireshark make it possible to see precisely what is going on in an HTTP/2 session.

Using the `tshark` command you can get output like the following:

```
$ tshark port 443 and host www.example.com
Capturing on 'Wi-Fi'
    1   0.000000 TCP 78 65277→443 [SYN] Seq=0 Win=65535 Len=0 MSS=1460
          WS=32 TSval=1610776917 TSecr=0 SACK_PERM=1
    2   0.096399 TCP 74 443→65277 [SYN, ACK] Seq=0 Ack=1 Win=14480 Len=0 MSS=1460
          SACK_PERM=1 TSval=2815107851 TSecr=1610776917 WS=128
    3   0.096489 TCP 66 65277→443 [ACK] Seq=1 Ack=1 Win=131744 Len=0
          TSval=1610777007 TSecr=2815107851
    4   0.096696 SSL 264 Client Hello
  ...
   33   0.386841 TCP 66 65277→443 [ACK] Seq=1043 Ack=7845 Win=128160
          Len=0 TSval=1610777288 TSecr=2815108131
   34   0.386842 TCP 66 [TCP Window Update] 65277→443 [ACK] Seq=1043
          Ack=7845 Win=131072 Len=0 TSval=1610777288 TSecr=2815108131
   35   0.386887 TCP 66 65277→443 [ACK] Seq=1043 Ack=9126 Win=129760
          Len=0 TSval=1610777288 TSecr=2815108131
   36   0.436502 HTTP2 143 HEADERS
   37   0.535887 TCP 1514 [TCP segment of a reassembled PDU]
   38   0.536800 HTTP2 1024 HEADERS, DATA
   39   0.536868 TCP 66 65277→443 [ACK] Seq=1120 Ack=11532
          Win=130112 Len=0 TSval=1610777433 TSecr=2815108271
```

This example dump gives you visibility into TCP, TLS, and HTTP/2. Other options[12] allow you to dig deep into all of those items to see precisely what is going on.

Summary

You can use the tools described in this chapter for quick tasks like verifying if your existing certificate includes the required h2 ciphers, low-level debugging of the HTTP communication, or setting up a simple h2 web server for more advanced testing. Knowing how to do these types of things will help you learn more about h2 and aid you in the transition of your website to the h2 protocol.

---

12 *https://www.wireshark.org/docs/man-pages/tshark.html*

CHAPTER 9

What Is Next?

We may have had a 20-year gap between HTTP/1.1 and HTTP/2, but from the looks of the current state of experimentation and research it seems unlikely we will see another decades-long break between versions. There is work going on even as adoption of h2 rises that is likely going to produce the next great thing in the world of internet protocols. To understand where this rapid iteration is coming from and the ideas behind it, it is important to have a bit of a background on the stack HTTP is built on.

TCP or UDP?

This is a debate you hear a lot these days, and though the question is valid it is also misleading. We discussed TCP in Chapter 3 when looking at the underlying motivations behind h2. To quickly recap, TCP is an IP datagram–based protocol that provides an agreed concept of a connection, reliability, and congestion control. These are the elements that allow TCP to be dependable and work consistently in a crowded internet. UDP (User Datagram Protocol), on the other hand, is much more basic. In this protocol datagrams (packets) are individual with no relation to any other UDP packet. There is no "connection," no guarantee of delivery, and no ability to adapt to different network conditions. It is perfect for building simple protocols like DNS that have small individual queries and small responses.

In order to make an application based on UDP be something that our next generation web can be built upon, we need to implement the idea of a connection, introduce reliability, and have some sort of congestion control. In other words, we need to reimplement much of what TCP already give us. So, if at the packet level these two protocols are mostly similar, and given the fact that in order for UDP to be useful for browsers we need to reimplement much if not all of the TCP stack, what is the motivation for a move from TCP to UDP? Why not just make changes to TCP and be done with it?

The answer has to do with where TCP is implemented. Most modern operating systems have their TCP stack in the kernel. It was long ago placed there for performance reasons. Changing the kernel is difficult, however. It is not something that a developer of the next great browser can generally do on her own. Kernel changes come from the operating system vendor and require an OS update to take effect. Since updating an operating system is a very high-overhead task when compared to upgrading your browser, the inertia of such a change is large enough to make such changes few and far between. When you consider that in order to work properly, much of the infrastructure on the internet would have to be updated as well, you can see that though revising TCP may be possible, it is not terribly practical.

So why would someone want to essentially reimplement the TCP stack in user space based on UDP? The short answer is control. By moving the TCP stack into user space —for example, in the browser itself—the developer gets unprecedented control over the network stack and can rapidly develop, deploy, and iterate new versions as quickly as people can auto-update their browsers. This is the experimenter's dream, and is the crux of the TCP versus UDP debate.

Thus the question should not be "TCP or UDP?" but rather "Kernel Space or User Space?" Keep that in mind the next time you hear someone extolling the virtues of one protocol over the other.

QUIC

Now that we have that debate out of the way we can intelligently discuss some of the technologies that are on the horizon, and even in use today.

One of the weaknesses of HTTP/2 is its reliance on popular TCP implementations. As discussed in "Inefficient use of TCP" on page 17, TCP connections are stuck in the cage of TCP slow start, congestion avoidance, and irrational reaction to missing packets. By placing all of the requests for all of the objects of a page on a single connection, you get the benefits of multiplexing, but you are vulnerable to the head of line blocking that can occur at the TCP level. A single TCP connection is still a great thing, but all great things can be improved upon.

QUIC, developed by Google, is an acronym for Quick UDP Internet Connection. QUIC takes HTTP/2, places it atop a user space resident UDP-based transport protocol (see "TCP or UDP?" on page 117), and folds in crypto, authentication, and other features to form a complete bundle of protocol goodness. Here is a description from the draft version of the RFC[1]:

---

1 *http://bit.ly/2pOEsaO*

QUIC provides multiplexing and flow control equivalent to HTTP/2, security equivalent to TLS, and connection semantics, reliability, and congestion control equivalent to TCP.

That is quite an impressive list. HTTP/2 put great effort into keeping the underlying TCP mechanism in place. QUIC leaves those constraints behind and makes a good thing better. Newton summed up this type of progress in 1676 when he said:

> If I have seen further, it is by standing on the shoulders of giants.
>
> —Sir Isaac Newton

QUIC has a number of important features that will help it pick up where h2 leaves off:

Out of order packet processing
> With h2 if a packet is lost on a TCP stream, the entire connection stalls until the packet is resent and received. QUIC will allow the application layer to continue to receive and process packets from streams that were unaffected by the loss.

Flexible congestion control
> QUIC's congestion control is designed to be pluggable. This will make it extremely easy to experiment with new algorithms or even swap in different algorithms depending on real-time conditions.

Low connection establishment overhead
> QUIC's goal is to have a zero round-trip time (0-RTT) connection establishment, including encryption and authentication. Using today's technologies (TCP and TLS 1.2) the minimum number of round-trips to establish a connection is three.

Authentication of transport details
> TCP is vulnerable today to injection attacks and similar concepts that take advantage of its trusting nature. QUIC will authenticate the packet header, making such attacks significantly more difficult (if not impossible).

Connection migration
> In a mobile and moving world, IP addresses may change during a long-lived connection. In a TCP world the connection will need to be broken down and reestablished. QUIC endeavors to make it possible to preserve connection semantics even when confronted by a moving client.

Though the RFC is not complete, a version of QUIC is available today in Chrome and many Google properties so you do not need to wait to try it out.

TLS 1.3

TLS (Transport Layer Security) is the Encryption and Authentication layer that HTTP/2 requires. Though it may feel that we only just moved to TLS 1.2, it is actually already approaching a decade since the RFC was published.[2] TLS 1.3 is currently in the works and as of March 2017 was at draft 19 of the RFC.[3] It represents a significant cleanup of TLS 1.2 and most importantly for our discussion addresses some performance-enhancing features while it shores up the protocol.

The most significant proposed improvement in TLS 1.3 is a 1-RTT for new connection (down from 3-RTT), and a 0-RTT for resumed connections. This trend can be summarized as "Round-trips are bad, let's eliminate them."

HTTP/3?

Will there be an HTTP/3? If so, what will it be?

The answer to the first question is undoubtedly, "yes." We are in a period of rapid experimentation and implementation of web protocols. Speed matters and has a direct effect on getting and retaining users on a website, which in turn has a direct effect on a site accomplishing its goals whether they be revenue generation, information dissemination, or human connection. In addition, implementors, web operators, and others are increasingly aware that though the internet may be a global phenomenon, internet access and quality vary greatly. Not everyone has a low-latency, high-bandwidth connection. That is all a grandiose way of saying that performance matters, and we will continue to work to approach the speed-of-light limitations of communications.

What will HTTP/3 be like is the more interesting question. HTTP/2 was inspired by the concepts in SPDY and used it as a starting point for its first draft. Will HTTP/3 do a similar thing with QUIC or will something new come along in the meantime that is better by all measures? We cannot say at this point, but it is fair to say that whatever coalesces into h3 will be faster, more reliable, more secure, and more resilient in more diverse internet conditions.

Summary

HTTP/2 is new. What that means is that the fun stuff is likely still to be discovered. We spent 20 years optimizing for HTTP/1—in fact, we built an industry around it. Some of the things that will feed into HTTP/3 are likely known, but it is probable that the best ideas are still out there to be discovered. Get out there and start using h2, push the boundaries, break things, learn—and when you are done, share. That is where HTTP/3 will come from.

---

2 *https://www.ietf.org/rfc/rfc5246.txt*

3 *https://tools.ietf.org/html/draft-ietf-tls-tls13-19*

HTTP/2 Frames

This appendix is a quick reference for the HTTP/2 framing layer. Each section includes the frame type number, the binary layout for the frame, a description of the frame, and a list of flags specific to that frame.

The Frame Header

As described in Chapter 5, each frame starts with the same nine bytes:

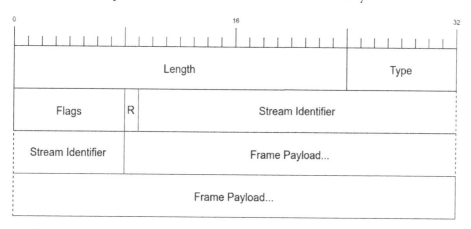

See Table 5-1 for a description of each field.

DATA

DATA frames contain arbitrary sequences of octets. This is a fancy way of saying these frames contain the requested/sent objects. Object data is split up across one or more frames depending on the maximum frame length. The padding length field and the padding itself are conditionally included to hide the size of the message for security purposes:

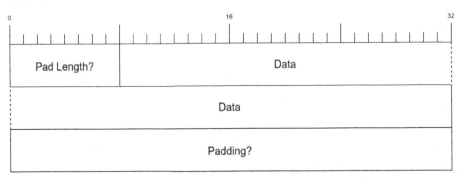

DATA Frame Fields

Name	Length	Description
Pad Length	1 byte	Indicates the length of the padding field. Will only be present if the PADDED flag is set in the frame header.
Data	Variable	The content of the frame.
Padding	Variable	Length set by the Pad Length field. All bytes are set to zero.

DATA Frame Flags

Name	Bit	Description
END_STREAM	0x1	Indicates this is the frame in the stream
PADDED	0x8	Indicates that the Pad Length and Padding fields are used

HEADERS

HEADERS frames are used to start streams and send message headers to an endpoint:

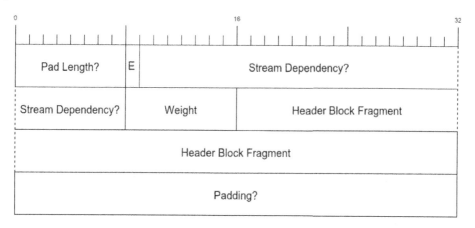

HEADERS Frame Fields

Name	Length	Description
Pad Length	1 byte	Indicates the length of the padding field. Will only be present if the PADDED flag is set in the frame header.
E	1 bit	Indicates whether the stream dependency is exclusive. Only present if the PRIORITY flag is set.
Stream Dependency	31 bits	Indicates which stream this stream is dependent on, if any. Only present if the PRIORITY flag is set.
Weight	1 byte	Indicates the relative priority of the stream. Only present if the PRIORITY flag is set.
Header Block Fragment	Variable	The headers for the message.
Padding	Variable	Length set by the Pad Length field. All bytes are set to zero.

HEADERS Frame Flags

Name	Bit	Description
END_STREAM	0x1	Indicates this is the frame in the stream.
END_HEADERS	0x4	Indicates this is the last HEADERS frame in the stream. If this is flag not set it implies a CONTINUATION frame is next.
PADDED	0x8	Indicates that the Pad Length and Padding fields are used.
PRIORITY	0x20	When set it indicates that the E, Stream Dependency, and weight fields are used.

PRIORITY

The PRIORITY frame is sent to indicate the priority of the stream. It can be sent multiple times and will change the advised priority if previously set:

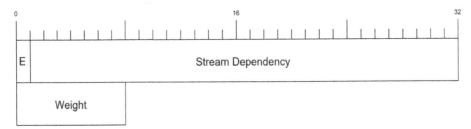

PRIORITY Frame Fields

Name	Length	Description
E	1 bit	Indicates whether the stream dependency is exclusive.
Stream Dependency	31 bits	Communicates the stream this stream is dependent on, if any.
Weight	1 byte	Indicates the relative priority of the stream.

A PRIORITY frame does not have any frame-specific flags.

RST_STREAM

RST_STREAM is used by either end of a stream to terminate the stream immediately. This is usually in response to an error condition.

The Error Code field in the frame is used to communicate the reason for the reset. See section 7 of RFC 7540[1] for a listing of those fields:

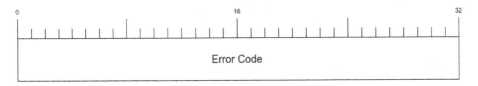

---

1 *https://tools.ietf.org/html/rfc7540#section-7*

SETTINGS

The SETTINGS frame is a sequence of key/value pairs. The number of pairs is defined by the frame length divided by the individual setting length (six):

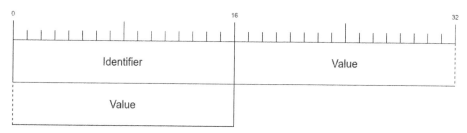

SETTINGS Parameters

Name	ID	Default	Description
SETTINGS_HEADER_TABLE_SIZE	0x1	4096	Changes the maximum size of the header table used for HPACK.
SETTINGS_ENABLE_PUSH	0x2	1	If set to 0 the peer may not send a PUSH_PROMISE frame.
SETTINGS_MAX_CONCUR RENT_STREAMS	0x3	No limit	Indicates the maximum number of streams that the sender will allow.
SETTINGS_INITIAL_WINDOW_SIZE	0x4	65353	Indicates the sender's initial window size for flow control.
SETTINGS_MAX_FRAME_SIZE	0x5	16384	Indicates the maximum frame size the sender is willing to receive. This value must be between this initial value and 16,777,215 (2^{24-1}).
SET TINGS_MAX_HEADER_LIST_SIZE	0x6	No limit	This setting is used to advise a peer of the maximum size of the header the sender is willing to accept.

When an endpoint receives and processes a SETTINGS frame, it must return a SETTINGS frame with the ACK flag (0x1) set in the frame header. This is the only flag defined for the SETTINGS frame. In this way the sender gets acknowledgment that the endpoint received the new SETTINGS and should be abiding by them.

PUSH_PROMISE

The PUSH_PROMISE frame is sent by a server to indicate to the client that it is about to send an object that the client has not explicitly requested. It is effectively the complement to a HEADERS frame sent by the client:

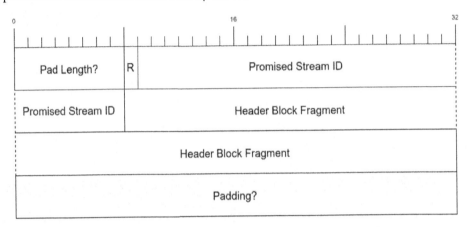

PUSH_PROMISE Frame Fields

Name	Length	Description
Pad Length	1 byte	Indicates the length of the padding field. Will only be present if the PADDED flag is set in the frame header.
R	1 bit	A single reserved bit. Do not set this or else.
Promised Stream ID	31 bits	Communicates the stream ID that the sender will use (will always be an even number as this is coming from the server by definition).
Header Block Fragment	Varible	The pushed headers for the message.
Padding	Variable	Length set by the Pad Length field. All bytes are set to zero.

PUSH_PROMISE Frame Flags

Name	Bit	Description
END_HEADERS	0x4	Indicates this is the last HEADERS frame in the stream. If this is not set it implies a CONTINUATION frame is next.
PADDED	0x8	Indicates that the Pad Length and Padding fields are used.

PING

The PING frame is intended to be used to measure the round-trip time between end-points. The frame has one flag, ACK (0x1). When an endpoint receives a PING frame without an ACK sent, it must send a PING frame back with the ACK flag set and the same opaque data. It should be noted that PING frames are not associated with any particular stream (they are connection level), and thus should have their stream identifier set to 0x0:

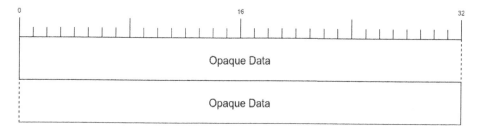

GOAWAY

The GOAWAY frame is used to gracefully shut down a connection. This is a connection-level frame and must be sent on stream identifier 0x0. By sending a GOAWAY frame, the endpoint is able to clearly define to the receiver what it has and has not received and what problem (if any) may have contributed to the GOAWAY. In the case of a problem, the error code will be set to one of the codes defined in section 7 of RFC 7540, and the Last Stream ID will be set to the highest stream ID that was processed. If there has been no error but the endpoint is about to tear down the connection (browser tab closed, connection timer exceeded, etc.), it sends the NO_ERROR (0x0) code and sets the Last Stream ID to 2^{31-1}:

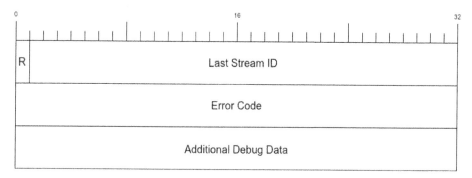

GOAWAY Frame Fields

Name	Length	Description
R	1 bit	A single reserved bit.
Last Stream ID	31 bits	The highest number stream ID the GOAWAY sender has received/processed. By sending this the receiver knows precisely what the sender has and has not received.
Error Code	4 bytes	The h2-defined error code or NO_ERROR code in the case of a successful shutdown.
Additional Debug Data	Variable	Opaque data the sender may send to indicate more information into the state or any problems.

WINDOW_UPDATE

The WINDOW_UPDATE frame is used for stream flow control. Sending a WINDOW_UPDATE frame to a peer tells that peer how many bytes the sender is willing to accept at that time. Flow control can apply to individual streams or all streams on a connection (Stream ID 0x0). Note that a WINDOW_UPDATE on a specific stream applies to the connection-level flow control as well:

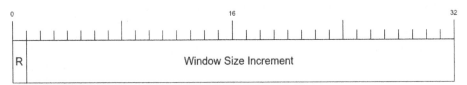

WINDOW_UPDATE Frame Fields

Name	Length	Description
R	1 bit	A single reserved bit.
Window Size Increment	31 bits	The number of bytes to increase the current window by.

The WINDOW_UPDATE frame has no frame-specific flags.

CONTINUATION

The CONTINUTATION frame contains additional headers from a previous HEAD-
ERS, PUSH_PROMISE, or CONTINUATION frame:

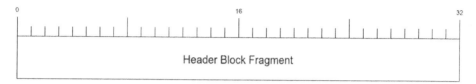

CONTINUATION Frame Fields

Name	Length	Description
Header Block Fragment	Variable	See HEADERS frame for a description.

CONTINUATION Frame Flags

Name	Bit	Description
END_HEADERS	0x4	Indicates this is the last HEADERS frame in the stream. If this is not set it implies another CONTINUATION frame is next.

Tools Reference

All of the tools referenced in the book are an internet search away, but for easy reference, a general sense of completeness, and an additional opportunity to date the writing of this book, here it is all in one place.

Tools

Application	URL
openssl	*https://www.openssl.org/*
nghttp2	*https://nghttp2.org/*
cURL	*https://curl.haxx.se/*
h2i	*https://github.com/bradfitz/http2/tree/master/h2i*
Wireshark	*https://www.wireshark.org/*
Certbot	*https://certbot.eff.org/*

Browsers

Application	URL
Microsoft Edge	*https://www.microsoft.com/en-us/windows/microsoft-edge*
Chrome	*https://www.google.com/chrome/*
Firefox	*https://www.mozilla.org/en-US/firefox*
Safari	*http://www.apple.com/safari/*
Opera	*https://www.opera.com/*

Servers, Proxies, and Caches

Application	URL
h2o	*https://h2o.examp1e.net/*
Apache	*https://httpd.apache.org/*
Squid	*http://www.squid-cache.org/*
IIS	*https://www.iis.net/*
nginx	*https://www.nginx.com/*
varnish	*https://varnish-cache.org/*
Jetty	*http://www.eclipse.org/jetty/*
Caddy	*https://caddyserver.com/*
Apache Traffic Server	*https://trafficserver.apache.org/*

Index

Request for Comments (RFCs), 3
request headers, 20
resource consolidation, 30
Responsive Web Design (RWD) sites, 29
RFC (Request for Comments), 3
Round Trip Time (RTT), 14
RST_STREAM frames, 124

S

Secure Socket Layer (SSL), 15
self-signed certificates, 8
server loads, 35
Server Push, 53-55, 66, 72, 92, 101-104
servers, choosing, 94-95
SETTINGS frame, 43, 125
sharding, 30, 36-37, 81
Single Point Of Failure (SPOF), 77
SPDY, 4, 43, 56
SPOF-O-MATIC, 77
spriting, 30, 37, 82
Stadium Effect, 20
start render time, 15
stream ID, 53
streams, 47-53
    flow control, 51
    messages, 48-51
    PRIORITY frames, 52-53
supporting older clients, 38
Switching Protocols response, 42, 51
SYN, 14
synthetic testing, 71

T

TCP (Transmission Control Protocol), 17-20
    connection optimization, 23-24

versus UDP, 117-118
TCP packets, 17-20
TCP sockets, 16
text compression and minification, 26
3rd Party Trailing Ratio, 21
third parties, 76-81
third-party content, 38
third-party objects, 20
three-way handshake, 14
Time to First Byte (TTFB), 15, 74-75
Time to Live (TTL), 24
Transport Layer Security (TLS), 15, 34-36
    browser support, 91
    negotiation time, 15, 16
    TLS 1.3, 119
    TLS Everywhere, 8
    and Wireshark, 116

U

UDP versus TCP, 117-118
unique domains/hostnames, 23
Upgrade header, 42

W

web browsers (see browsers)
web page requests, 11-13
Web Page Test (WPT), 69, 71, 84, 109
web performance (see performance)
web servers, 9, 94-95
WINDOW_UPDATE frames, 51, 128
Wireshark, 115-116

Y

yahoo.com performance testing, 86-88

About the Authors

Stephen Ludin is Chief Architect for Akamai's Web Performance division. He runs Akamai's Foundry team, a research and development group focused on the web technologies of tomorrow. He serves on the board of the Internet Security Research Group (parent organization for Let's Encrypt), as well as Rubicon Labs.

Ludin received his degree from the University of California at San Diego in Computer Music, where his coding abilities were used in writing C programs to create experimental music. The world is a better place for his decision to use his creative, technical, and management skills in a more aesthetically pleasing realm of making the web a faster and safer place for commerce and communications.

Javier Garza is a multilingual technology evangelist who loves taking things apart, understanding how they work, and finding the best/most practical way of improving them. He started hacking BASIC-based computer games at the age of 9, and has been working with computers for the past 25 years in Spain, Germany, and the US (half that time at Akamai helping the largest websites on the internet run faster and more securely).

Colophon

The animals on the cover of *Learning HTTP/2* are golden-mantled ground squirrels (*Callospermophilus lateralis*). They are part of the *Sciuridae* family and are abundant in the western portion of North America where they can survive in forests, meadows, and dry flatland environments.

The golden-mantled ground squirrel can be easily confused with a chipmunk due to their similar appearances. Both have black stripes that run down their back, but those stripes do not reach the face on the squirrels. The squirrels are also larger in size (ranging from 9 to 12 inches long) and weigh between 4 and 14 ounces. The squirrels have longer tails than their chipmunk brethren, and white rings of fur around their eyes. They get their name from the brownish fur atop their heads.

Golden-mantled ground squirrels are omnivorous and collect food in pockets in their mouths. They need to store up enough fat to survive hibernation in the winter. Their diet includes seeds, fruit, insects, fungi, bird eggs, and even small veterbrates. They will save some of this food for when they wake in the spring time and emerge from their hibernation burrows.

Breeding for the golden-mantled ground squirrel typically takes place during the spring months. Males usually emerge from hibernation before females, so breeding won't start until both parties are available. Gestation lasts around 28 days with females giving birth to hairless litters of around 5 babies. Pups will start to wean and become independent three to six weeks after birth.

Many of the animals on O'Reilly covers are endangered; all of them are important to the world. To learn more about how you can help, go to *animals.oreilly.com*.

The cover image is from *Pictorial Museum of Animated Nature*. The cover fonts are URW Typewriter and Guardian Sans. The text font is Adobe Minion Pro; the heading font is Adobe Myriad Condensed; and the code font is Dalton Maag's Ubuntu Mono.

Learn from experts.
Find the answers you need.

Sign up for a **10-day free trial** to get **unlimited access** to all of the content on Safari, including Learning Paths, interactive tutorials, and curated playlists that draw from thousands of ebooks and training videos on a wide range of topics, including data, design, DevOps, management, business—and much more.

Start your free trial at:
oreilly.com/safari

(No credit card required.)

CPSIA information can be obtained
at www.ICGtesting.com
Printed in the USA

33164300085243   /P
June 2017